MW00389599

Four Views of the End Times
Participant Guide

Timothy Paul Jones, PhD

This Participant Guide accompanies the

Four Views of the End Times 6-Session DVD-Based Study
(ISBN 9781596364127 or ISBN 9781596364240)

with

Four Views of the End Times Leader Guide
(ISBN 9781596364257)

PUBLISHING

© 2010 Bristol Works, Inc.
Rose Publishing, Inc.
4733 Torrance Blvd., #259
Torrance, California 90503 U.S.A.
Email: info@rose-publishing.com
www.rose-publishing.com

Angel photo ©Peter Zelei

Scripture taken from *The Holy Bible, English Standard Version.* Copyright © 2000; 2001 by Crossway Bibles, a division of Good News Publishers. Used by permission. All rights reserved.

Printed in the United States of America

Contents

SESSION ONE **9**
The Goal of God's Plan
Get This: Keep your eyes on the right end.

SESSION TWO **19**
Four Ways to End the World
Get This: Learn to look for common ground.

SESSION THREE **39**
Kingdom Already, Kingdom Not Yet: Amillennialism
Get This: Because of the death and resurrection of Jesus, Satan is already defeated.

SESSION FOUR **55**
Building a Better World: Postmillennialism
Get This: Never underestimate the power of the gospel!

SESSION FIVE **71**
Rapture Ready? Dispensational Premillennialism
Get This: Always be ready for the return of Jesus.

SESSION SIX **87**
Through Tribulation to Everlasting Life: Historical Premillennialism
Get This: God grows his people through trials and tribulations.

Meet the Author

Thanks for picking up your copy of Four Views of the End Times! My name is Timothy Paul Jones, and I live in Louisville, Kentucky, with my wife Rayann and our daughter Hannah—as well as one over-energetic Siberian Husky. I'm a professor, but over the past two decades, I've had the privilege of serving as a pastor in several wonderful congregations of believers, most recently at First Baptist Church of Rolling Hills in Tulsa, Oklahoma. In these contexts, I saw over and over how theology and church history could help people to flesh out their faith in powerful ways.

Now, I serve as professor of church ministry at one of the largest seminaries in the world, The Southern Baptist Theological Seminary in Louisville, Kentucky. Here, I invest my time in mentoring a rising generation of God-called ministers of the gospel. I also edit the *Journal of Family Ministry* and write books in the fields of history, apologetics, and family ministry. I enjoy spending time with my family, walking along tree-lined streets, reading neglected books, drinking French-pressed coffee, and cooking for students and friends. Our family is involved in children's ministry at the east Louisville campus of Sojourn Community Church.

Thanks for your willingness to walk alongside me in this study! If you enjoy Four Views of the End Times, I encourage you to continue the conversation with me by aiming a tweet in my direction at http://twitter.com/4ViewsoftheEnd or by digging into my book *Christian History Made Easy*.

About This Study

"Tell us," the disciples asked Jesus after their master had predicted a future calamity in Jerusalem, "when will these things happen? What will be the sign of your coming and of the end of the age?" (Matthew 24:3). The dodgy dozen weren't the first or the last folk to ask such questions. In every generation since sin entered into the world, God's people seem to have wondered, "When and how will God make things right in the world?"

Sometimes these discussions degenerate into fruitless debates about specific details—but that's not where Dr. Timothy Paul Jones will take you in this particular study. Although you will gain much knowledge about the end times, the primary purpose of this study is not to raise your eschatological I.Q. This study focuses first and foremost on Jesus the Messiah, the One through whom God the Father will make all things new. Woven through this study of Jesus in Revelation, you will find straightforward, Scripture-centered examinations of four viewpoints that Christians throughout history have embraced as they looked toward the end of time.

About the Complete Four Views of the End Times
DVD-Based Small Group Kit
(ISBN 9781596364127)

The Kit includes everything you need to teach *Four Views of the End Times*, using professionally-produced video sessions and a PowerPoint® presentation. The Complete Kit includes:

- DVD with 6 teaching sessions, as well as optional Q&A segments

- One printed *Four Views of the End Times Participant Guide* (ISBN 9781596364264)

- One printed *Four Views of the End Times Leader Guide* (ISBN 9781596364257) + PDF Leader Guide

- One *Four Views of the End Times* pamphlet with side-by-side comparisons of each view (ISBN 9781596360891)

- *Four Views of the End Times* CD-ROM with optional PowerPoint® presentation (ISBN 9781596363014)

- PDF files for posters, fliers, handouts and bulletin inserts for promotion

Available at www.FourViewsoftheEndTimes.com or
www.rose-publishing.com, or by calling Rose Publishing at 1-800-532-4278.
Also available wherever good Christian books are sold.

Quick Summary of the Four Views

Amillennialism

There will be no (a-) physical millennium. The millennium is the present, spiritual reign of Jesus with his people. Jesus may return to earth at anytime. The tribulation occurs whenever Christians are persecuted or wars and disasters happen.

Postmillennialism

Jesus will return to earth after (post-) a millennium when the overwhelming majority of people throughout the world embrace the gospel. The great tribulation occurred either in the first-century AD, or will be a brief time of persecution immediately preceding the millennium.

Dispensational Premillennialism

God will rapture Christians from the world before (or midway into) the seven-year great tribulation. Jesus will return to earth after the great tribulation, but before (pre-) the thousand-year millennium described in Revelation 20.

Historical Premillennialism

Jesus will return to earth after a time of tribulation, but before (pre-) the millennium described in Revelation 20. Christians will remain on earth through the tribulation. This tribulation may be a short, intense time of persecution that will occur near the end of time, or a long time-period which has occurred throughout church history.

The Goal of God's Plan

Get This:

Keep your eyes
on the right end.

Session 1 Outline
The Goal Of God's Plan

1. If we focus on the wrong end, the end times can be:

    a. Confusing

    b. Dangerous

    c. Even violent

2. Focus on the right end—Jesus

    a. Revelation 22:13

        • Jesus is the beginning and the end

        • Arius denied that Jesus is the beginning and end

    b. Acts 1:6–8

        • Jesus' followers got focused on the wrong end

    c. Matthew 28:19–20

        • Jesus provided his people with a mission

3. Jesus is the end point and goal of God's work in history

End-Times Craziness

This is a dangerous study. It's a study about the end of time, after all. It's a journey to the end of the world. This is the stuff of prophetic placards, apocalyptic films, and frightening visions.

What's more, a quick glance at history shows that studying the end times has the capacity to bring out a bit of craziness from time to time.

- Not too many years after Jesus rose from the dead, a few false prophets in Thessalonica caused all sorts of consternation when they proclaimed that Jesus had already returned (2 Thessalonians 2:2).

- A century later, in the mid-100s, a man named Montanus became a believer in Jesus and developed a strong interest in prophetic themes. Before long, Montanus had predicted that the New Jerusalem would soon show up in Pepuza, a backwoods parish in the province of Phrygia. Before being disfellowshipped, Montanus even claimed that he spoke for the Holy Spirit, declaring, "I am Father, Word, and Comforter" and "I am the Lord God All-Powerful." (Didymus, *De Trinatate*, 3:41; Epiphanius, *Hæreses*, 48:11)

- Almost a millennium and a half later, in 1534, a Dutch baker named Jan Matthys claimed that the New Jerusalem would soon be located in Münster, Germany. After a supposed series of apocalyptic visions, Jan and his followers subjugated the city of Münster. One of Jan's cohort married 16 wives and even declared himself a successor of the biblical King David. In the end, the New Jerusalem did not arrive in Münster, but a rival army did. The corpses of the apocalyptic revolutionaries were suspended above the city in iron cages. To this day, those cages still hang from the steeple of St. Lambert's Church, silent reminders of an apocalyptic expectation gone desperately wrong. (A. Arthur, *The Tailor King*; St. Martin's, 1999; pp. 67, 103–164)

- Three hundred years later, Joseph Smith claimed that Jesus would establish the New Jerusalem in Missouri—and, in the process, launched a worldwide religious movement that denied essential biblical truths about Jesus. To this day, members of the Mormon religion expect the return of Jesus to entail the establishment of an "American Zion" on the eastern outskirts of Kansas City, Missouri.

But, in recent years, such shenanigans have ended, haven't they? Surely postmodern people are sufficiently enlightened not to fall for these claims about the end times! If that's what you're thinking, think again.

- Fast-forward to the twentieth century: In the late 1980s, one leader in an apocalyptic sect changed his name to David Koresh and urged his disciples to think of themselves as "students of the Seven Seals" in Revelation. (J. Curl, "Davidians, friends gather in Waco to praise Koresh," *The Washington Times*, April 20, 2003). Koresh embraced polygamy and claimed that the end-times prophecies of Daniel would be fulfilled at his communal compound near Waco, Texas. In 1993, David Koresh and 75 of his followers perished after a 51-day siege of the compound. (K.G.C. Newport, *The Branch Davidians of Waco*; Oxford, 2006; pp. 155–339)

- Even more recently, there have been doomsday expectations surrounding the year 2000, one prediction that Jesus would return on May 21, 2011, and several claims connected to the year 2012. (J. Berton, "Biblical scholar's date for rapture" http://articles.sfgate.com/2010-01-01/bay-area/17466332_1_east-bay-bay-area-first-time-camping)

See what I mean? Studying the end times can quickly turn crazy. And, sometimes, studying the end of time can even turn dangerous. But don't pitch this book back into the box quite yet! There's a crucial fact that you need to know about studying the end of time: It's only hazardous when you focus on the wrong end.

Keeping Your Eyes on the Right End

*"I am the Alpha and Omega, the first and the last, the beginning
and the end."—Revelation 22:13 ESV*

According to Scripture, the end of time is not the ultimate end or goal of God's plan. In fact, the endpoint of the divine plan is not any temporal event at all. The endpoint and goal of God's work in human history is Jesus. Jesus is the source of the created order (John 1:3; Colossians 1:16). He is, in the words of the Nicene Creed, the one "by whom all things were made." Yet Jesus is more than the source of God's story; he is also the goal of all that God is doing. He is not only the beginning but also the end. And how should we respond to this truth? By "fixing our sight on Jesus, the captain and completer of our faith" (Hebrews 12:2). Jesus is the ultimate goal of God's plan. That's why the biblical authors could describe the entire time between Jesus' victory over death and the end of time as "the last days" (Acts 2:17; Hebrews 1:2).

- When you planned to participate in this study, what did you expect to learn about the end times?

_____

_____

_____

- Was this initial expectation focused on "the right end" or "the wrong end"?

_____

_____

_____

- In Revelation 22:13, John described Jesus as "the Alpha and Omega, the first and the last, the beginning and the end." Who did John present as "Alpha and Omega" in Revelation 1:8 and 21:1–7?

Alpha and Omega

These are the first and the last letters of the Greek alphabet. John used these terms to identify Jesus as God and to describe Jesus as both the beginning and the goal of God's work in human history.

_____

_____

_____

- Now compare the words of John with ancient prophecies found in Isaiah 41:4 and 44:6. What does this suggest to you about who John understood Jesus to be?

_____

_____

_____

- Study Acts 2:14–18 and Hebrews 1:1–2. According to these passages, how long have believers in Jesus been living in "the last days"?

_____

_____

♰ Look up and read Acts 1:4–8

- Read carefully the question about the kingdom that came from the followers of Jesus. What event were these early followers of Jesus eagerly anticipating?

_____

_____

_____

_____

> ### Nicene Creed
>
> The Nicene Creed is the confession of faith that developed from the creeds of the Councils of Nicaea (AD 325) and Constantinople (AD 381). At these councils, Christian leaders agreed that the eyewitnesses of Jesus' life, death, and resurrection had understood Jesus to be fully human yet fully and uniquely God.

- What event did Jesus want his followers to anticipate?

_____

_____

_____

- How did the apostles want or expect Jesus to respond to their question?

_____

_____

- Judging from the response of Jesus, where did he want his followers to focus their concerns?

_____

_____

Focusing on the Goal of God's Plan

Whenever the precise order of events at the end of time becomes our primary focus, we are focusing on the wrong end. A few folk may respond to such a false focus by seeking an increasingly specific schedule for the termination of time. Still fewer may gravitate toward extremist cults. But, even among the most stable individuals, the results of fixing our eyes on the wrong end are far from the best. Such a focus tends to lead us toward tension, anxiety, and a desire to stockpile more and more details about the end times.

But how might our perspective change if we fix our eyes on the right end? What happens when we focus on Jesus as the goal of God's plan? How might this refocusing reshape our studies of the end times? The apostle Paul provided a partial answer when he wrote to a church that was struggling to comprehend God's plan for the end of time. Immediately after clarifying some issues that church members had misunderstood, Paul pointed to this hope: "May our Lord Jesus Christ himself and God our Father, who loved us and gave us eternal comfort and good hope through grace, comfort your hearts and establish them in every good work and word" (2 Thessalonians 2:16–17).

It is true that, when Jesus was asked about events related to his coming in judgment, Jesus may have given his followers a few signposts. Yet the closing parable of this same discourse made it clear that his primary concern was not for them to have a detailed understanding of each event. His desire was for them to be prepared whenever the end might come (Matthew 24:3, 42–51).

Even after his resurrection, when the apostles demanded details about the end of time, Jesus replied quite curtly, "It is not for you to know times or seasons that the Father has fixed in his own authority"—then, he immediately reminded them of their responsibility to share with others what they had seen in him (Acts 1:8).

In some cases, in-depth studies of the end times have resulted in painful divisions and quarrelsome discussions among God's people. And yet, according to the book of Hebrews, the result ought to be precisely the opposite: "Let us encourage one another—and all the more as you see the Day approaching" (Hebrews 10:25). Did you catch that? As believers in Jesus become more aware of the nearness of the Day of the Lord, the more they should encourage one another! If your study of the end times leaves you discouraged and divided, it's quite likely that you have focused your attention on the wrong end.

- Have you ever become too focused on the specific events that may accompany the end of time? Or do you have a friend who became too focused on the details of end-times events? What were the results?

_____

_____

_____

- During this study of the end times, what will you do to center your thinking on Jesus?

_____

_____

_____

Where This Study is Going

From the words of Jesus and Paul, it seems that the result of studying the end times should not be a fleeting consolation that comes from knowing more details about the future. Instead, where our study should drive us is toward a simultaneous sense of rest and responsibility that is found only through the gospel of Jesus. The result should not be increased speculation about the end of time but an increased capacity to work for the glory of Jesus the Messiah while watching and waiting for his return.

That's why my goal in this study is not merely for you to know more about the end times. Instead, my desire is for you to know more of the One whose arrival fulfills a divine design that is more ancient than time. If you signed up for this study looking for formulas to calculate the day when time will end, you are likely to be disappointed. If your heart is hungry for Jesus, my hope is that you will be satisfied far beyond your wildest dreams, because Jesus is the goal and endpoint of God's plan for history. If the end of time is a puzzle, Jesus is the corner pieces. Only when Jesus stands in the most prominent places can the end-times puzzle begin to make sense.

At this point, I must warn you again, though: Increased anticipation of the glory of Jesus may end up being dangerous—but not in any way that will land you in the middle of an apocalyptic cult. It's dangerous because, whenever Jesus becomes central, life-as-usual ends up disrupted. Where the glory of Jesus is central, the allures of consumerism and self-centered goals and the culture's profile for success lose their luster. This is dangerous in the same way that Jesus himself was dangerous:

> **Messiah**
>
> (from Hebrew *Mashiakh*, "Anointed One") He is Savior-king anticipated throughout the Hebrew Scriptures (Genesis 3:15; Deuteronomy 18:15; Isaiah 53; 61). Also known as "Christ" (from Greek *Christos*, "Anointed One")

It's dangerous because, once Jesus truly shows up, nothing can remain the same as it was before. And so, if you want a comfortable life that places you in control, you'd be better off quitting this study now—or spending each session focused on the details of the end of time. If you want the revolution that God offers to you in Jesus, leap into this study with a focus on Jesus, whenever and however he may choose to return.

Now What?

PRAY: Jesus our Messiah and God our Father—you who grant eternal comfort and good hope through your grace—plant your gladness, your joy, and your Spirit firmly in my heart. Establish me in every good work and word as I await the return of Jesus. In the name of Jesus, I pray. Amen (Based on 2 Thessalonians 2:16–17).

LEARN: Study Acts 1:1–8 and Revelation 22:12–17. Memorize Revelation 1:1–2.

Do: Apply Acts 1:8 in your life this week. Write on a 3x5 card:, "Because Jesus is the endpoint of history, the end is always near, and his message must be my mission." Place the card in a prominent location in your home or vehicle. Each time you see the card, pray for an opportunity that day to live in the Holy Spirit's power by telling someone you meet about what Jesus has done in your life.

> **Jesus**
>
> Jesus is the goal and the endpoint of God's work in human history.

Four Ways to End the World

Get This:

Learn to look for common ground.

Session 2 Outline
Four Ways to End the World

1. The book of Revelation is apocalyptic

   a. Contains visions and extravagant imagery

   b. Arose from the Jewish community

   c. Uses numbers symbolically

2. Revelation is *not* pseudepigraphical writing

   a. Written by the apostle John

3. Two times that Revelation could have been written:

   a. Emperor Nero (AD 54–68)

   b. Emperor Domitian (AD 81–96)

4. The opening of Revelation

    a. To the seven churches

    b. God the Almighty (Pantokrator)

    c. Three key things in Revelation

        • Tribulation

        • Kingdom

        • Patient endurance

5. Four ways Christians view the end of time

    a. Historical Premillennialism

    b. Dispensational Premillennialism

    c. Amillennialism

    d. Postmillennialism

Key Terms

Amillennialism There will be no ("a-") physical millennium. The millennium is the present, spiritual reign of Jesus with his people.

Apocalyptic Literature Genre of ancient Jewish literature presented in the form of visions that figuratively pointed to hidden truths for the purpose of assuring God's people of the goodness of God's plans during periods of persecution.

Asia Minor Region also known as Anatolia, comprising most of the modern nation of Turkey (see Map of Asia Minor).

Dispensational Premillennialism God will "rapture" Christians from the world before the great tribulation. Jesus will return to earth after the great tribulation, before ("pre-") the millennium described in Revelation 20.

Domitian Ruled the Roman Empire, AD 81–96. According to the ancient historian Suetonius, "Domitian issued an encyclical in the name of his governors that declared 'Our Master and our God bids that this be done.'" (Suetonius, *Vita Domitianus*, 13:2)

Eschatology Study of the events leading up to the end of time. From Greek *eschaton* ("final" or "last") and *logos* ("word" or "idea").

Historical premillennialism Jesus will return to earth before ("pre-") the millennium described in Revelation 20, following a time of tribulation.

John the Elder The earliest references to the authorship of Revelation suggest that John the apostle wrote the Gospel of John as well as Revelation and probably 1 John. In the fourth century, Eusebius suggested that the apostle John and John the Elder might be two different people and that John the Elder may have written 2 John, 3 John, and Revelation. The fact that the author of Revelation presents himself simply as "John" (Revelation 1:4) and speaks with authority as a representative of Jesus suggests that John the apostle wrote the book of Revelation and that the same "John" was both the apostle and the elder.

Nero Ruled the Roman Empire, AD 54–68. After a fire in Rome, a rumor circulated that Nero had started the fire. According to the ancient historian Tacitus, "To get rid of this report, Nero accused and inflicted exquisite tortures on a class hated for their abominations, the ones called Christians." (Tacitus, Annales, 15:44) This persecution seems to have been limited to the regions around Rome.

Pantokrator / Autokrator The Roman emperor was known as autokrator ("sole ruler"). Pantokrator means "all ruler" or "almighty." In Revelation 1:8, John refers to God as pantokrator.

Patmos Island off the west coast of Asia Minor. According to Tacitus, people who threatened the peace of the Roman Empire were sent to coastal islands such as Patmos. Fourth-century church historian Eusebius reported that Emperor Domitian exiled John in AD 95. Eighteen months later, after Domitian's death, John was allowed to leave the island (see Map of Asia Minor).

Postmillennialism Jesus will return to earth after ("post-") a millennium when the overwhelming majority of people throughout the world embrace the gospel.

Pseudepigrapha Writings ascribed to individuals who could not possibly have written the book. Often times, the ascribed author lived hundreds of years before the time the book was actually written. The book of Revelation is not pseudepigraphical because John lived during the time Revelation was written.

Seven Churches of Revelation The churches in Asia Minor to which John addresses the book of Revelation. The churches are: Ephesus, Smyrna, Pergamum, Thyatira, Sardis, Philadelphia, and Laodicea (see Map of Asia Minor).

Map of Asia Minor

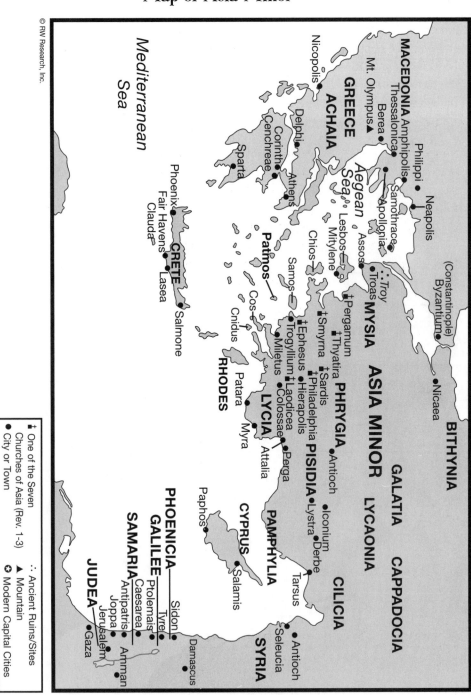

© RW Research, Inc.

✝ One of the Seven
Churches of Asia (Rev. 1-3)
● City or Town

∴ Ancient Ruins/Sites
▲ Mountain
✪ Modern Capital Cities

Mediterranean Sea

MACEDONIA
Nicopolis
Mt. Olympus▲
GREECE
ACHAIA
Delphi
Corinth
Cenchreae
Sparta
Athens
Amphipolis
Thessalonica
Berea
Samothrace
Apollonia
Philippi
Neapolis
Aegean Sea
Lesbos
Mitylene
Chios
Samos
Patmos
Cos
Cnidus
Phoenix
Fair Havens
Clauda
CRETE
Lasea
Salmone
RHODES
Patara
Myra
LYCIA
Attalia
Perga
Assos
∴Troy
Troas
MYSIA
✝Pergamum
✝Thyatira
✝Smyrna
✝Ephesus
Trogyllium
Miletus
Hierapolis
✝Sardis
✝Philadelphia
✝Laodicea
Colossae
PHRYGIA
PISIDIA
Antioch
Iconium
Lystra
Derbe
ASIA MINOR
GALATIA
LYCAONIA
CAPPADOCIA
(Constantinople)
Byzantium
Nicaea
BITHYNIA
CYPRUS
Paphos
Salamis
PAMPHYLIA
Tarsus
CILICIA
Antioch
Seleucia
SYRIA
PHOENICIA
GALILEE
SAMARIA
JUDEA
Ptolemais
Caesarea
Antipatris
Joppa
Jerusalem
Gaza
Sidon
Tyre
Damascus
Amman

Revelation as Apocalyptic

Even if you don't know a lot about the Bible, one thing becomes quite clear as you read the book of Revelation: It is very different from other books in the New Testament! Revelation refers to historic events—but it isn't a historical text like the Gospels or Acts. The book includes letters to seven churches—but these letters aren't anything like the correspondence that Paul sent to churches throughout the Roman Empire.

So why is the book of Revelation so different from other New Testament texts? The book of Revelation draws from an ancient literary style known as apocalyptic [ah-POKK-ah-LIPP-tikk]. The word "apocalyptic" comes from the Greek *apokalupsis* ("revelation"), a term that also happens to be the first word in the Greek text of Revelation! Apocalyptic writings included visions that figuratively pointed to hidden truths for the purpose of assuring God's people of the goodness of God's plans during periods of persecution. In Revelation, the primary hidden truth that is revealed is the centrality of Jesus in all of history.

Parts of Daniel and Ezekiel in the Hebrew Scriptures are also written in apocalyptic style. Plus, there are apocalypses that do not appear in any Hebrew or Christian Scriptures at all—one that falsely claims to come from Enoch, for example, and others that allege origins in the lifetimes of Moses and Noah. Revelation is not completely apocalyptic, but several common apocalyptic traits do appear in the book of Revelation.

- After carefully reading the definition of "apocalyptic literature," glance through the books of Ezekiel and Daniel in your Bible. Based on the definition provided here, which chapters in Ezekiel and Daniel seem to be apocalyptic?

_____

_____

_____

Apocalypse Now—and Then

There have tended to be four approaches to biblical apocalypses. Some people read apocalyptic literature futuristically, others read it historically or idealistically, while others take a preterist perspective. None of these four approaches completely excludes the others. In fact, nearly every interpreter of the end times draws from more than one of these approaches when reading biblical books such as Daniel and Revelation.

❧ Four approaches to interpreting apocalyptic literature

Futurist	A futurist treats the text as a predictive prophecy about events that, even now, have not yet occurred. If I read Revelation futuristically, I search for predictions in Revelation to help me to understand events that will occur near the end of time.
Historicist	Historicism treats apocalyptic writings as symbolic retellings of certain epochs of history; if someone reads Revelation in this way, that person might assume, for example, that John is using lavish language to retell the rise and fall of the Roman Empire or some other series of historical events.
Idealist	When read idealistically, apocalypses are seen as symbolic expressions of struggles between good and evil that occur in every age. If idealism makes the most sense to you, you would treat each scene in Revelation as a symbol of some ongoing conflict between the reign of God and the powers of evil. Such struggles will continue until the end of time.
Preterist	The word "preterist" comes from the Latin *praeteritus* ("past" or "bygone") and suggests that most or all the events described in apocalyptic text have already passed. A preterist reading of an apocalyptic writing understands the text to describe events that happened near the time when the text was written. There are two types of preterists: (1)Orthodox preterists (also known as partial preterists) interpret some visions in Revelation as descriptive of events in the first century AD, but they also recognize other portions of the book—particularly descriptions of the return of Jesus to earth—as futurist. (2)Full preterists think that biblical prophecies describe only events that happened in the first century. According to full preterists, Jesus has already returned to earth spiritually, and he will not actually return to earth in any physical way. Full preterism is a heresy that rejects truths clearly found in Scripture and in the ancient creeds. Orthodox Christians throughout history have refused to accept full preterism.

In the chart on the four approaches, highlight or underline key words that will help you to remember each approach to apocalyptic literature.

Look up and read Revelation 1:1–8

In Revelation 1:1, "soon" may imply that, while some events described in Revelation remain in the future, many aspects of John's prophecy occurred soon after John wrote this text. The word could also mean "quickly" or "without warning."

• Do some research and determine the most appropriate meaning for the word "soon" as it is used in Revelation 1:1. Write your conclusion in the space below:

_____

_____

_____

In Jewish apocalyptic literature, the number seven almost always pointed to "completeness." The phrase "seven spirits" (1:4) probably refers to the completeness or sufficiency of the Holy Spirit. This phrase might be paraphrased as "sevenfold Spirit" or "all-sufficient Spirit." The task of the Holy Spirit is to testify to the truth that is found in Jesus (John 15:26).

• What does it mean for your daily life to say that the Holy Spirit is "complete" or "sufficient"?

_____

_____

_____

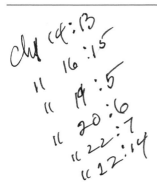

What approaches might this view take to ...

	... the 7 churches in Revelation? (Rev. 1–3)	... the great tribulation? (Rev. 4–19)	... the millennial kingdom? (Rev. 20)	... the new creation? (Rev. 21–22)
Amillennialism	**Orthodox Preterist:** John was describing seven actual churches in the first century. **Idealist:** Each church symbolized a type of church that can be found in every age.	**Historicist:** Describes distresses that God's people have endured throughout history. **Orthodox Preterist:** Describes first century persecutions and conflicts. **Idealist:** Symbolizes distresses that God's people endure in every age.	**Idealist:** Symbolizes the reign of Jesus in the lives of his people. **Historicist:** The reign of Jesus through his people from the establishment of the church to the end of time.	**Futurist:** God will glorify all who trusted Jesus and condemn all who rejected him.
Postmillennialism	**Orthodox Preterist:** John was describing seven actual churches in the first century. **Idealist:** Each church symbolized a type of church that may be found in every age.	**Historicist:** Describes distresses that God's people have endured throughout history. **Orthodox Preterist:** Described first-century persecutions and conflicts. **Idealist:** Symbolizes distresses that God's people endure in every age. **Futurist:** Describes a time of distress immediately before the millennium begins.	**Historicist:** The reign of Jesus through his people. **Futurist:** Describes a future time when Jesus begins to reign through his people.	**Futurist:** God will glorify all who trusted Jesus and condemn all who rejected him.

	... the 7 churches in Revelation? (Rev. 1–3)	... the great tribulation? (Rev. 4–19)	... the millennial kingdom? (Rev. 20)	... the new creation? (Rev. 21–22)
Dispensational Premillennialism	**Orthodox Preterist:** John was describing seven actual churches in the first century. **Historicist:** Each church represents an era of church history.	**Futurist:** Describes a seven-year time of distress between the rapture and Jesus' return to establish his millennial kingdom.	**Futurist:** Describes a future time when Jesus will physically reign on earth.	**Futurist:** God will glorify all who trusted Jesus and condemn all who rejected him.
Historical Premillennialism	**Orthodox Preterist:** John was describing seven actual churches in the first century. **Idealist:** Each church represented a type of church that may be found in every age.	**Historicist:** Describes the distresses that God's people have endured throughout history. **Orthodox Preterist:** Described first-century persecutions and conflicts. **Idealist:** Symbolizes distresses that God's people endure in every age. **Futurist:** Describes a time of distress immediately before Jesus returns to establish his millennial kingdom.	**Futurist:** Describes a future time when Jesus will physically reign on earth.	**Futurist:** God will glorify all who trusted Jesus and condemn all who rejected him.

Unveiling Through Visions:
The content of apocalyptic literature

Ancient apocalypses claimed to unveil divine truths that could not be discovered through human effort. Like other apocalypses, the book of Revelation presents fantastic visions that use mysterious language and numbers to point to larger realities. Unlike other apocalyptic writings, what is revealed first and foremost in Revelation is not a plan but a person. Over and over, Jesus stands at the center of John's visions. Jesus is the Lion and Lamb who breaks the Seven Seals (Revelation 5–8). It is he who takes his stand on Mount Zion (14:1) and he who embraces his people as his beloved bride (19:7). In the end, Jesus is the conquering King of kings, the Lord of lords, and the light who illumines his people's lives forevermore (17:14; 21:23; 22:3). From the very first sentence, the book of Revelation is a revelation "of Jesus Christ" (Revelation 1:1). (For *Iesou Christou* in Revelation 1:1 as subjective genitive, see George Eldon Ladd, *A Commentary on the Revelation of John*; Eerdmans, 1972)

Encouragement During Persecution:
The context of apocalyptic literature

Apocalyptic writings developed during times of exile or persecution. That's clear even in the first verses of Revelation: There, John described himself as "your brother and co-participant in the tribulation and the kingdom and the patient endurance in Jesus… on the island called Patmos on account of the word of God and the witness of Jesus" (1:9). In some cases, the apocalyptic literary style concealed elements of the message that the dominant political powers might have perceived as subversive. John seems to have written Revelation either during the reign of Emperor Nero in the AD 60s or in the AD 90s when Emperor Domitian ruled the Roman Empire.

Here are a few reasons why many scholars place Revelation in the reign of Domitian: In the first place, the second-century writer Irenaeus of Lyons—a student of Polycarp, who knew the apostle John—recollected that John had penned Revelation during Domitian's reign. (Irenaeus, *Adversus Haereses*, 5:30:3) Furthermore, Revelation seems to have been written at a time when Christians in the cities of Asia Minor were experiencing harassment for their faith (Revelation 1–3). In the 90s, Domitian did indeed persecute families around Rome for their refusal to recognize him as divine. Pressure to worship the emperor as "Lord and God" probably spread to Asia Minor. An image of the emperor even seems to have been constructed in the city of Ephesus, in Asia Minor. (G.K. Beale, *The Book of Revelation*; Eerdmans, 1999; p. 712) (See map on page 24)

A strong case can also be made for a date in the mid-60s, however. Scholars who place Revelation in Nero's reign emphasize how, in Revelation 11, John speaks of the Jewish temple as a present reality, as if the temple was still standing. The Roman army burned the temple in Jerusalem in AD 70. On this basis, these scholars contend that the book must have been written before that time, probably during the reign of Nero.

Assurance of God's Goodness:
The purpose of apocalyptic literature

When people today read apocalyptic literature, the first question that is often asked is, "What will be the precise order of events between now and the end of time?" When apocalyptic writings first circulated, however, that probably wasn't people's primary question. What readers then were likely asking was not what or how but who: "Who's really in charge of history?"

When Daniel proclaimed his prophecies, for example, it seemed like the Babylonians, Medes, and Persians controlled the world. To many Israelites, it looked as if God was no longer working for the good of his people. Through divinely-disclosed visions, Daniel made it clear that God's kingdom was "an everlasting kingdom" and that Israel's oppressors would one day be condemned to "everlasting contempt" (Daniel 2:44; 4:3, 34; 12:2). What God provided through Daniel's prophecies was hope rooted in eschatology—an assurance that God was working in a definite direction and, in the end, God would make all things good, right, and new.

When John wrote Revelation, the Roman Empire ruled the known world. Christians were losing their positions, their property, and even their lives because they refused to offer sacrifices on the emperor's behalf. The Jewish faith remained legal—albeit unpopular—in the Roman Empire. As a result, some Christians may have downplayed their trust in Jesus and tried to blend in at local synagogues (see Revelation 2:9; 3:9).

In this context, John proclaimed that the rightful king of the world was not the emperor in Rome; Jesus was the King of kings, and his power extended far beyond the heavens to encompass every kingdom on earth (11:15; 21:23). Like Daniel, John also offered his readers eschatological assurance and hope:

Not only was God working even in times of persecution, someday God would consign his foes to a pit of fire, re-create the fallen cosmos once and for all, and wipe every tear from his people's eyes (20:12–21:8).

- What does the word "eschatology" mean?

_____

_____

- Who or what stands at the center of John's eschatology?

_____

_____

- Name at least one essential truth that Christians must believe about the end of time.

_____

_____

Looking for the common ground

So what are the essential truths that Christians must believe about the end of time? The ancient Apostles' Creed declares that Jesus "ascended to the right hand of God the Father; from there, he will return to judge the living and the dead." Later in the same creed, Christians state their belief in "the resurrection of the body, and the life everlasting." The Nicene Creed echoed and expanded this essential confession: "He ascended into heaven and is seated at the right hand of the Father. He will come again in glory to judge the living and the dead, and his kingdom will have no end. ... We await the resurrection of the dead, and the life of the world to come." Regardless of their view of the end times, Christians throughout the world and throughout time share this common confession: Jesus who was crucified returned to life, ascended to his Father, and will return physically to earth.

The Themes that Matter Most:
Kingdom, Tribulation, and Patient Endurance

"I, John, your brother and partner in the tribulation and the kingdom and the patient endurance that are in Jesus, was on the island called Patmos on account of the word of God and the testimony of Jesus."—*Revelation 1:9 ESV*

KINGDOM

The overwhelming majority of Christians throughout church history have agreed that God the Father inaugurated a kingdom in the life, death, and resurrection of Jesus. The good news of Jesus is, after all, the good news of the kingdom! (Matthew 3:2; 4:17, 23). Another term for the kingdom of God is "the kingdom of heaven"; when we compare parallel passages in the Gospels, it is very clear that the kingdom of God and the kingdom of heaven are two different phrases that describe one identical reality (compare Matthew 8:11 with Luke 13:29, or Matthew 11:11 with Luke 7:28).

> *The kingdom of God is God's people living in God's domain under God's rule.*
>
> (G. Goldsworthy, *Gospel and Kingdom*; Paternoster, 1994; ch. 5)

TRIBULATION

At the same time, Christians recognize that this Christ-inaugurated kingdom has not yet been fully realized on earth. God's people experience persecution, tribulation, and distress. All creation "groans together" with the children of God (Romans 8:22). One day, the kingdom that the Father inaugurated in Jesus will be consummated so completely that, for those who have taken their stand with Jesus, every form of tribulation will end.

PATIENT ENDURANCE

Until the consummation of the kingdom, Christians wait and work with patient endurance. Patient endurance is very different from laziness or passive waiting. Patient endurance means working together to express and to expand the kingdom of Christ in the lives of people around us while patiently resting in the goodness of God's providence here and now.

* Describe each of the three key themes in your own words:

  Kingdom _____

  _____

  _____

Tribulation_____

_____

_____

Patient endurance _____

_____

_____

Why Study the End Times?

By this point, perhaps you have asked yourself, "If there's so much common ground among Christians, why are there different views of the end time? Why can't everyone agree on one perspective?" These are good questions, but they aren't easily answered! The entire issue would be far simpler if all Bible-believing Christians held one particular view while all slanderers of Scripture pursued other perspectives. But that's simply not the case when it comes to studying the end times. When it comes to the study of eschatology, Christians who sincerely trust the truth of Scripture have arrived at very different perspectives. That's been the case at least since the second or third century and will probably continue until the end—at which time God might prove us all wrong!

Why then should we even study the end time? Why not simply be "pan-millennialists" who say, "It will all pan out in the end"? Or how about "pro-millennialists" who declare, "Whenever God does it, I'm for it"? Why concern ourselves with differing perspectives on the end of time? Here's why: As you study the differences between each perspective, you will become more able to distinguish which issues in eschatology really matter most. As you begin to understand each view, you will develop richer and deeper perspectives on how God may consummate his kingdom at the end of time. Perhaps most important of all, as you learn to appreciate others' perspectives, you should find yourself focusing less on particular end-times events and more on how each viewpoint exalts Jesus.

With that in mind, here are four primary perspectives on the end times that have emerged throughout the history of Christianity. All four of these views have been held by people who authentically trust Jesus and accept the truth of Scripture. Most important, all four perspectives agree that Jesus rose from the dead, ascended to his Father, and will someday return physically to judge all humanity.

Amillennialism:	There will be no ("a-") physical millennium. The millennium is the present, spiritual reign of Jesus with his people.
Postmillennialism:	Jesus will return to earth after ("post-") a millennium when the overwhelming majority of people throughout the world embrace the gospel.
Dispensational Premillennialism:	God will rapture Christians from the world before the great tribulation. Jesus will return to earth after the great tribulation, before ("pre-") the millennium described in Revelation 20.
Historical Premillennialism:	Jesus will return to earth before ("pre-") the millennium described in Revelation 20, following a time of tribulation.

So how and why have Christians developed such dissimilar perspectives on the end of time? Remember the three themes that we considered earlier? Kingdom, tribulation, and patient endurance. On the point of patient endurance, all four views stand together: Christians should patiently endure distress. Where the views diverge is in the precise nature and relationship of the other two themes: kingdom and tribulation.

All four viewpoints recognize that God's people endure trials and tribulation—but when it comes to the great tribulation described in Revelation 7 and in Jesus' end-times discourse with his disciples (Mark 13), the perspectives begin to differ. Dispensational premillennialists place the return of Jesus for his church immediately before a seven-year great tribulation. Other perspectives treat the great tribulation as a representation of distresses that God's people have experienced throughout the ages or as a description of conflicts that happened in the first century.

People from all four perspectives agree that the kingdom of God will be fully consummated at some point in the future. But when it comes to the millennial kingdom described in Revelation 20, each viewpoint turns a slightly different direction. From the perspective of amillennialists and some postmillennialists, the millennial kingdom is a present, spiritual reality. For historical premillennialists, the kingdom is both a present experience and a future, physical reality. According to dispensational premillennialists, the modern state of Israel will still receive all the land that God promised Abraham.

As you study each millennial perspective, notice carefully how each one differs when it comes to the great tribulation and the millennial kingdom. As you pay attention these differences, pay even closer attention to how each viewpoint exalts Jesus.

• Which view of the end times makes the most sense to you right now? Locate at least one Scripture that seems to support this perspective.

_____

_____

_____

• Which view of the end times makes the least sense to you right now? Try to find at least one Scripture that could support this perspective.

_____

_____

_____

It's Not Just about the Future

Kingdom. Tribulation. Patient endurance. If you are a believer in the Lord Jesus, these three themes are not simply theoretical aspects of your future life. They are woven into every moment of your life here and now. You have confessed Jesus as the king of all kings. Yet your gas tank still gets empty, your baby's diaper still gets full, and some months still outlast the balance in your checking account. What's more, sometimes you still struggle to submit yourself to the Messiah's reign in your life. Other times, you may be treated unjustly because of your faith in Jesus.

And so, what do you do? You patiently endure tribulation; you rejoice in God's ever-present presence while never ceasing to pray, "Your kingdom come, your will be done, on earth as it is in the heavens." The themes of kingdom, tribulation, and patient endurance are as near to you as the events of this very day. What are you doing to expand God's kingdom here and now? How are you responding to times of tribulation? And where do you need to learn what it means to endure distress with patience?

Now What?

Pray: "Heavenly Father, reign in me so that I reflect your kingdom. Messiah Jesus, work in me so that I glorify you even in times of tribulation. Sevenfold Spirit, reveal through me your perfection and sufficiency. God in Three Persons, to your name be the glory. Amen."

Learn: Read chapters 1, 2, and 3 in the book of Revelation. Look for the themes of kingdom, tribulation, and patient endurance in John's letters to the seven churches. Memorize Revelation 1:9.

Do: In the space below, list three areas of life in which you need to learn "patient endurance." This week, in each of these areas, seek specific ways to submit this area of your life to the kingship of the living Lord Jesus.

1. _____

2. _____

3. _____

Kingdom Already, Kingdom Not Yet: Amillennialism

Get This:

Because of the death and resurrection of Jesus, Satan is already defeated.

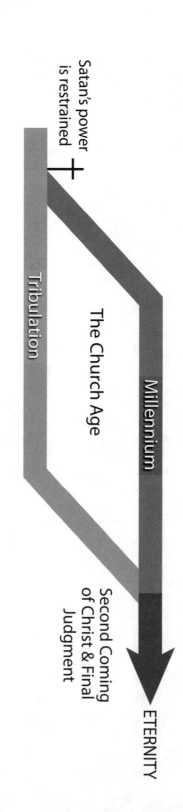

Amillennialism

Satan's power
is restrained

Tribulation

The Church Age

Millennium

Second Coming
of Christ & Final
Judgment

ETERNITY

Session 3 Outline
Kingdom Already, Kingdom Not Yet: Amillennialism

1. Amillennialism

    a. Already, but not yet complete

    b. Millennium is the spiritual reign of Jesus

2. Numbers

    a. Symbolically express spiritual truths

    b. Not a literal 1,000-year millennium

3. Progressive Parallelism

    a. 42 months; Revelation 11:1–2; 13:5

4. Satan has been bound

    a. Revelation 5:1–7

    b. Revelation 20:1–2

    c. John 12:31–32

    d. Colossians 2:15

    e. Luke 10:18

    f. Matthew 12:29

5. Jesus is already the victor

Key Terms

Amillennialism There will be no ("a-") physical millennium. The millennium is the present, spiritual reign of Jesus with his people.

Apocalyptic Literature Genre of ancient Jewish literature presented in the form of visions that figuratively pointed to hidden truths for the purpose of assuring God's people of the goodness of God's plans during periods of persecution.

Augustine of Hippo (AD 354–430) North African bishop and widely influential theologian. Often identified as an amillennialist—possibly the first—although some of his theology was similar to postmillennialism.

Four Living Creatures Revelation 5:6. Probably angelic creatures similar to cherubim (Ezekiel 10:14) and seraphim (Isaiah 6:1–3). In Jewish tradition, the eagle, bull, lion, and man represented the four mightiest creatures. These four angelic creatures—perhaps like "four winds" and "four corners" of the earth (Revelation 7:1; 20:8)—may represent the powers of the created order. (L. Morris, *The Book of Revelation, InterVarsity,* 1987; page 89)

Numbers From an amillennialist perspective, numbers in apocalyptic literature don't necessarily represent actual time periods or literal quantities. Instead, they symbolically express spiritual truths. For example, 7=completeness, 6=incompleteness, 12=people of God, and 1,000=a great time or magnitude.

Progressive Parallelism Literary pattern in which an author describes an event or series of events, then moves backward and retells some of these events before moving forward. A clear example of this pattern, also known as recapitulation, can be found in Genesis 1:1–2:25. Amillennialists see such overlaps in apocalyptic literature.

Tribulation Not an exact 42-month time period, but any time of testing, purifying, and calling to repentance. Tribulations occur since the time of Jesus to the end of time.

Twenty-Four Elders (1) Angelic council, perhaps guardians of Israel and the church, that surrounds the throne of God. Scripture describes a council of angelic beings around the divine throne (1 Kings 22:19; Psalm 89:7). White clothing is often the garb of angelic creatures (Matthew 28:3; Acts 1:10), and "elders" functions as a title for angels (Isaiah 24:23). (2) Heavenly expression of the 24 groups of priests and Levites who praised God in the Jerusalem temple (1 Chronicles 24:4; 25:9–31). (3) Symbol of God's people dwelling in eternal glory, pointing to Israel's twelve patriarchs and the church's twelve apostles, similar to Revelation 21:12–14 where the names of tribes and apostles are inscribed on the eternal city.

Between D-Day and V-Day

On June 5, 1944, Dwight Eisenhower rode to an airfield near the English village of Newbury. There, thousands of Allied paratroopers were preparing to plummet from airplanes above France, landing several miles behind Nazi lines. Eisenhower wished the troops well and watched as their transports lifted from the runway. When Eisenhower returned to his vehicle, his driver saw tears in his eyes. It was expected that three-fourths of these men would die in the next twenty-four hours. Even as he waved his farewell to the transports, Eisenhower carried in his pocket a note that read, "My decision to attack at this time and place was based upon the best information available.... If any blame or fault attaches to the attempt it is mine alone." (S. Ambrose, *D-Day*; S&S, 1994; pp. 190–195. C. D'Este, *Eisenhower*; MacMillan, 2003; pp. 527–528. E. Larrabee, *Commander-in-Chief*; S&S, 1988; p. 455)

During the first bloody days after the D-Day invasion, it seemed to some military strategists that Eisenhower might need to release this admission of defeat. And yet, fifty days later, the Allies still held the beaches at Normandy. By summer's end, Nazi commanders found themselves scissored between the Allied Expeditionary Force in France and the Russian army in Eastern Europe. In one sense, once the Nazi armies were forced to fight on two fronts instead of only one, the war in Europe was over. Yet the victory remained far from complete! The liberation of Paris, the Battle of the Bulge, and the Berlin Strategic Offensive Operation had yet to occur. Many lives were lost, and a final triumph still seemed uncertain at times. In the months between D-Day and V-Day, victory in Europe was already and not yet. The turning point of the war had already been reached and Hitler's fall was inevitable, but the moment of surrender had not yet been reached. (O. Cullmann, *Christ and Time*; Westminster, 1950; p. 84)

The Kingdom of God—Already and Not Yet

Already and not yet—that's how amillennialism treats the time between the resurrection of Jesus and the end of time. Through the death and resurrection of Jesus, God has already triumphed over darkness and established his eternal kingdom. Jesus defeated Satan through the cross and empty tomb. Ever since that victory, the millennial kingdom has been present in the reign of God with his people in the heavens. Still, the complete consummation of God's kingdom has not yet occurred; so, until Jesus returns, times of tribulation will still transpire on the earth. For amillennialists, the millennial kingdom of Jesus is not something that will happen in the future. The millennial kingdom is happening right now. Even during times of tribulation, the millennial kingdom endures, particularly in God's present reign through the saints who are already with him in glory.

A broad range of believers—including many who strongly embrace Scripture as God's Word—have identified themselves as amillennialists. The fifth-century church father Augustine of Hippo was an amillennialist, though some aspects of his thinking were similar to postmillennialism. More recently, students of Scripture ranging from J.I. Packer and Jay Adams to Herschel Hobbs and Hank Hanegraaff have taken an amillennial perspective on the end of time.

The tag "amillennial" isn't quite accurate, unfortunately—the prefix "a-" means "not," suggesting that amillennialists don't believe in a millennium at all! In fact, amillennialists do believe in a very real millennial reign. They simply understand the millennial kingdom to be a present spiritual reality rather than a future earthly event.

Revelation by the Numbers

"But wait!" someone is probably saying right now. "According to Revelation, doesn't the millennium last one thousand years? If Revelation says that the millennium lasts a thousand years, how can the millennium stretch from the time of Jesus to the end of time? That's been almost two thousand years already!" And indeed, Revelation 20:4 does describe a divine reign that endures for a thousand years. How then can a thousand years possibly refer to the reign of Jesus through his people from his resurrection until his return?

According to amillennialists, this is possible because "a thousand years" wasn't intended to describe a specific length of time; it was meant to describe an idea—in this case, the greatness of God's reign. John did not—from an amillennial perspective—intend the numbers in Revelation to be read as precise statistics. John, like other apocalyptic writers, used numbers to point to certain concepts or ideas. If amillennialists are correct, what John intended when he wrote "a thousand years" was not a precise time-period but simply a reign of great magnitude or length.

⸆ What might the numbers suggest in apocalyptic literature?

Number	Possible meaning	Examples
1,000	Great length or magnitude	Ezekiel 47:3–5; Revelation 20:1–7
42	Cleansing through tribulation (perhaps suggestive of human incompleteness, 6, multiplied by divine completeness, 7)	Revelation 11:2; 13:5; 42 encampments in the wilderness, Numbers 33:5–29; perhaps 42 months in Luke 4:25; James 5:17
12	The people of God	Ezekiel 47:13; Revelation 12:1; 21:12–21
10	Something significant or extreme but limited	Daniel 7:7, 20–24; Revelation 2:10
7	Completeness	Ezekiel 39:9, 12, 14; Daniel 4:23; Revelation 5:6
6	Incompleteness	Revelation 13:18; perhaps Daniel 3:1
4	Earthly powers	Daniel 7:2–3, 17; 8:8; 11:4; Revelation 7:1

• Look carefully at the chart of numbers and the possible meanings. If John intended the numbers in his apocalyptic text to be read with meanings such as these, how might that change your reading of Revelation?

_____

_____

_____

Seven Facets of a Single Truth

Another important aspect of amillennialism also concerns how John intended his words to be read. People working from other millennial viewpoints sometimes treat Revelation as a series of prophecies that must occur in the same chronological order that they appear in the book.

Amillennialists, however, suggest that John wrote Revelation in progressive parallelisms. If God did guide John to write Revelation in progressive parallelisms, here's how the book seems to be structured: John told and retold one inspired truth—that God will judge evil and vindicate those who trust Jesus—seven times in seven ways through seven different sections. The first of these sections is found in Revelation 1–3, the second appears in chapters 4–7, followed by chapters 8–11, then 12–14, 15–16, 17–19, and finally 20–22. John marked the end of each parallel section by making specific reference to eternal blessedness or divine judgment. Each section in Revelation represents a different facet of one single glorious fact: One day, God will glorify his people and destroy every remnant of sin. The tribulations and judgments described in each section will not occur consecutively at the end of time; they happen simultaneously throughout human history.

The Last Days
The reign of Chirst from heaven that began at the time of his death, burial, ressurection, and ascension

The Last Days
The end of time, when the present created order gives way to new creation and Christ returns in glory.

Revelation 20-22

Revelation 18-19

Revelation 15-17

Revelation 12-14

Revelation 8-11

Revelation 4-7

Revelation 1-3

The seven parallel sections are also progressive. What that means is that each section moves forward a little further than the one before. The second section speaks more clearly about the end of time than the first, and the third section inches closer to the end than the second section, and so on, until the seventh section clearly reveals God's consummate triumph.

Such parallelisms occur in other ancient texts too—and not only in apocalypses! In Genesis, for example, the initial account of creation ends with God resting on the seventh day (Genesis 2:1–3). Then, in Genesis 2:4–25, the author of Genesis went back to the sixth day and retold the creation of humanity in more detail before moving forward to the temptation of humanity in Genesis 3. That's progressive parallelism.

Amillennialists suggest that God revealed the visions of Revelation in a similar fashion. In each section, John picturesquely depicted divinely-inspired truths about God's kingdom, judgment, and tribulation; then John backed up, retold the same truths in more detail, and moved forward—until finally, in the seventh section, John saw the glorious end of all time, when the final victory becomes clear and complete! In that day, God will turn D-Day into V-Day, and the already will overwhelm every fragment of the not yet.

- Take a few moments to look at the progressive parallelism in Genesis 1–2. Then, survey the book of Revelation. Study each of the seven suggested sections in Revelation. What is the greatest strength of reading Revelation as progressive parallelism?

_____

_____

_____

- Do you see any weaknesses in viewing God's revelation to John as a progressive parallelism? If so, what are they?

_____

_____

_____

℘ Look up and read Revelation 5:1–7

First-century readers of Revelation would have recognized immediately what sort of document John was describing here: It was a will or testament. In the ancient world, wills were "written within and on the back," "sealed with seven seals" (5:1), and opened when someone died (5:6) to be executed by someone specially qualified or appointed (5:5). (G. Beale, *The Book of Revelation*; Eerdmans, 1999; p. 344)

What the Lamb opens in this text is nothing less than the eternal will of God. Because Jesus died and rose from the dead, the living one who enacts the will of God is also the one whose death made it possible to open the will. The slaughtered Lamb is also the royal Lion and the risen Lord! It is through the one Lord that the "seven spirits of God"—or the "sevenfold Spirit of God," emphasizing the Spirit's perfection—proceeds throughout "all the earth" (5:6).

- Why was "no one … worthy … in heaven or on earth or under the earth" (5:3–4) to open the scroll?

_____

_____

_____

- The elder declared that "the Lion … has conquered" (5:5). Who or what did Jesus conquer? How?

_____

_____

_____

(*See Key Terms for explanations of the Four Living Creatures and Twenty-Four Elders.*)

What on Earth Was Going on When John Wrote Revelation?

Read from an amillennial viewpoint, Revelation 5 describes how Jesus—through his obedient death and triumphant resurrection—was revealed as worthy to enact God's will. The breaking of each seal unleashes great calamities (Revelation 6–8). These events of tribulation represent sufferings that have occurred and will continue throughout the time between the resurrection of Jesus and his glorious return.

When John wrote these words, Christians throughout the Roman Empire were clearly experiencing many calamities that he described, especially if John wrote these words during the reign of Emperor Domitian. The first and second seals unleashed horsemen and brought conflict and war—and both messianic and non-messianic Jews were still reeling from those ghastly days in AD 70 when the Roman army burned Jerusalem, slaughtering and enslaving its citizens. The third and fourth seals brought forth famine. It's likely that many readers remembered the widespread starvation that followed a catastrophic failure of the grain harvest in AD 92.

The fifth seal produced persecution—another close experience for the first readers of Revelation, since either Domitian or Nero was bullying Christians for their refusal to worship the emperor. The sixth seal birthed seismic upheavals and darkness in the skies, calling to mind the great earthquakes that wracked the Roman Empire in AD 60 as well as the eruption of Mount Vesuvius in AD 79. Such events did not end in the New Testament era. Still today, war, famine, persecution, and natural disasters afflict our world.

Two times, the book of Revelation identifies a time of tribulation that lasts "forty-two months" (Revelation 11:2–3; 13:5). A few interpreters of Revelation understand these two references to forty-two months as two separate times of tribulation that will occur immediately after each other; this would result in a great tribulation that lasts seven years.

Amillennialists, however, understand the forty-two months as a single symbol that draws from the forty-two encampments of Israel in the wilderness (Numbers 33:5–29) and perhaps from the forty-two months of drought during the ministry of Elijah (Luke 4:25; James 5:17). Through forty-two wilderness encampments, Israel was purified; throughout forty-two months of drought, Elijah called people to repent. Likewise, through times of tribulation, the church is continually cleansed and non-believers are called to turn from their sin. Such tribulations occur throughout history.

The forty-two months is an important symbol. It points to a great tribulation that began with the Messiah's victory over Satan through the cross and empty tomb (Revelation 12:5–8) and that will continue until the end of time. The great tribulation is not only an event that will happen someday but also an event that has happened and is happening right now. The fact that these events originate in God's will (Revelation 5:1) and culminate in God's victory (19:1–20:15) stands as a glorious reminder that "for those who love God, all things work together for good" (Romans 8:28).

- Summarize in your own words how amillennialists understand "great tribulation."

_____

_____

_____

- List below at least three questions that you have as you consider the amillennial perspective.

_____

_____

_____

ℂ Look up and read Revelation 20:1–3

Through the work of Jesus upon the earth, Satan was thrown down (John 12:31–33). Because of this overthrow of Satan, the powers of darkness have been radically restrained (Colossians 2:15). Jesus has received from his Father power over death (Revelation 1:18; 9:1; 20:1). From an amillennial perspective, this restraining of Satan was what Jesus was describing when he said to his disciples, "I have been watching Satan falling like a flash from heaven. Look, I've given you authority to trample on snakes and scorpions, authority over every power of the hateful one! None of these powers—not even one—will do damage to you" (Luke 10:18–19).

To express this historical truth in apocalyptic language, John depicted an angelic representative of Jesus binding Satan and casting Satan into a pit (Revelation 20:2). The pit and the binding are metaphors for the shattering of Satan's power that occurred through the ministry of Jesus. The Lord himself used a similar metaphor to describe his work when he said, "No one can enter a strong man's house … unless he first binds the strong man" (Matthew 12:29; Mark 3:27).

And in what way might it be said from an amillennial perspective that Satan cannot "deceive the nations any longer"? (Revelation 20:3). Through the proclamation of the gospel to non-Jews, the message of God's truth moved beyond Israel to "the nations." Because this message is now available to Gentiles, Satan's power over the nations has been limited; he no longer rules the nations in the same way that he did when God's revealed Word remained the domain of Israel.

- Carefully study the passages below. In what ways did the work of Jesus bind or restrain the power of Satan?

Matthew 12:29 _____

_____

Luke 10:18–19 _____

_____

John 12:31–33 _____

_____

Colossians 2:15 _____

ℭ *Look up and read Revelation 20:4–6*

When Christians—including martyrs—die (20:4), they experience the first resurrection. Their spirits enter God's presence to reign with him as "priests of God and of Christ ... for a thousand years" (20:6; see 2 Corinthians 5:8). This thousand years represents the entire time from the resurrection of Jesus until his return. So, even though Jesus has not yet returned to earth, his millennial kingdom is already real and present in the heavens. Many amillennialists see the millennial kingdom as present both among deceased believers whose spirits are with God and among God's people on earth here and now (Luke 17:20–21).

- If amillennialism is correct, where is the millennial kingdom located right now?

_____

_____

_____

- In Revelation 20:1 which statements seem to support amillennialism?

_____

_____

_____

If amillennialism is correct, the next item on God's eschatological agenda is the moment when Jesus returns to resurrect and to judge all humanity (the second resurrection), to reveal to the world that Satan has already been defeated ("he must be released for a little while"), to relegate Satan to eternal torment (the lake of fire, 20:10), and to re-create his world (a new heaven and a new earth, 21:1). Once Jesus returns, eternity begins.

- If this became your view of the end times, what might change in your day-to-day habits of life?

_____

_____

_____

- Near the beginning of the study for this session, you listed elements of amillennial eschatology that didn't make sense to you. Even if you disagree with amillennialism, do you now have a better understanding of those elements? If so, what helped you to understand amillennialism better?

_____

_____

_____

Believing in the Already, Living in the Not Yet

Once the troops that landed in northern France on D-Day held the beaches near Normandy, there were still many battles to be fought. Yet, in one sense, VE-Day—the day of victory in Europe—became only a matter of time. In the same way, once Jesus defeated Satan on the cross, the ultimate victory of God became merely a matter of time.

You may not accept amillennialism as the best view of the end times—and that's okay! Even if you find yourself embracing some other eschatological viewpoint, amillennialism reminds Christians of an important theme in Scripture: Jesus has already won. To be sure, there are still trials and struggles and tribulations. Yet—through his perfect life, sacrificial death, and

> *Jesus has already won! Amillennialism emphasizes the present reality of the millennial kingdom and the victory of Jesus through his life, death, and resurrection.*

glorious resurrection—Jesus the Messiah has shattered Satan's power and won a kingdom for his Father. Final victory is only a matter of time.

Now What?

PRAY: Father, I praise you for forming your people into a kingdom of priests. I thank you that you have drawn me into this kingdom. On my own, I could never have imagined or deserved such grace. Guide me as I seek your glory and dominion in every part of my life. Help me to watch expectantly as you form a community for your glory, drawn from every tribe and nation in the name of Jesus the Messiah. Amen. (Based on Revelation 1:5–6.)

LEARN: Study chapters 4, 5, 6, and 7 in the book of Revelation. Memorize Revelation 7:9–10.

Do: God's desire and design is a many-colored kingdom from every culture. Jesus died on the cross to purchase "a great multitude from every nation from all tribes and peoples and languages" (Revelation 7:9). This week, look specifically for ways that you can begin preparing now for this divine design. How? Examine your biases and prejudices. Is there an ethnic group that you struggle to embrace? If so, ask God to change your heart in this area. Then, begin working to build a new relationship with a believer from an ethnic group or socio-economic background that's different from your own. If you do not know any believers from other ethnic or socio-economic backgrounds, earnestly ask God to bring such a person into your life.

Building a Better World: Postmillennialism

Get This:

Never underestimate the power of the gospel!

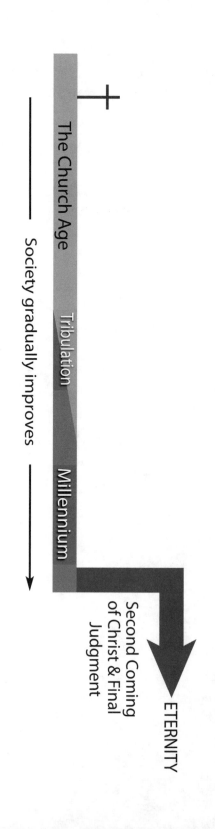

Postmillennialism

The Church Age

Tribulation

Millennium

Society gradually improves

Second Coming
of Christ & Final
Judgment

ETERNITY

Session 4 Outline
Building a Better World: Postmillennialism

1. Postmillennialism

   a. The transforming power of the gospel

2. Millennium

   a. Jesus will reign spiritually through the power of the gospel

   b. Physical return of Jesus occurs after the millennium

3. Tribulation

   a. Tribulation before the millennium, Matthew 13:31–33

   b. Jonathan Edwards: Tribulation was 1,260 years since the Pope rose to power

   c. Contemporary Postmillennialists:

      • Preterism

      • Nero, 666; Revelation 13:16–18

      • Destruction of the temple, AD 70; Revelation 11:1–2; Mark 13:1–2, 24–27

4. Proclaim the gospel and expect it to bring about a millennial kingdom

Key Terms

Destruction of the Temple After Emperor Nero committed suicide in AD 68, his general Vespasian claimed the throne and charged his son Titus to quell a Jewish rebellion in Jerusalem. Hundreds of thousands of Jewish persons were killed and enslaved during this conflict. Titus' soldiers looted and destroyed the temple in Jerusalem, as depicted in the Arch of Titus. Some postmillennialists see the Jewish-Roman War and the destruction of the temple in AD 70 as the fulfillment of Jesus' words in Matthew 24.

Gematria A system of assigning numerical values to letters, words, or phrases.

John Calvin (1509–1564) French author and pastor during the Protestant Reformation.

Jonathan Edwards (1703–1758) Theologian and pastor in New England during the Great Awakening modern mission movement."

Nero Ruled the Roman Empire, AD 54–68. After a fire in Rome, a rumor circulated that Nero had started the fire. According to the ancient historian Tacitus, "To get rid of this report, Nero accused and inflicted exquisite tortures on a class hated for their abominations, the ones called Christians." (Tacitus, *Annales*, 15:44) This persecution seems to have been limited to the regions around Rome.

Postmillennialism Jesus will return to earth after ("post-") a millennium when the overwhelming majority of people throughout the world embrace the gospel. Jesus will not be physically present on earth during the millennial kingdom.

Preterism (From Latin *praeteritus*, "past") View of New Testament prophecy that understands most events described in apocalyptic texts as predictions that were fulfilled in the first century. Some postmillennialists are also preterists.

Radical Preterism The belief that all biblical prophecies were fulfilled in the first century and that Jesus will never physically return to earth. Orthodox preterists recognize radical preterism as a heresy that must be rejected.

Theonomist Postmillennialism Also known as reconstructionist postmillennialism, the belief that, as part of the movement toward a millennial kingdom, the church should work to bring civil powers into submission to Old Testament Law. Some Charismatic Christians embrace a form of theonomist postmillennialism known as "dominion theology."

William Carey (1761–1834) English Baptist pastor and missionary to India; known as the "father of the modern mission movement."

A Powerful Gospel

Have you ever found yourself in awe at the power of the gospel? Perhaps it was in a worship service where a friend unexpectedly trusted in Jesus Christ. Maybe it was in a small group where you watched as the gospel shattered the stranglehold of addiction in someone's life. Perhaps it was in your own life when you saw how the cross of Jesus calls you to trade your bitterness for God's forgiveness. Whatever the setting, what you witnessed was the life-transforming power of the gospel. You caught a glimpse of good news that is powerful beyond all human imagination. According to the apostle Paul, the gospel is the power of God that restores wholeness in the lives of those who trust Jesus (Romans 1:16). This power-filled good news is not only how God rescues people from future condemnation but also how God grows and changes his people throughout their lives.

- Describe a time in your life when you saw firsthand the power of the gospel.

_____

_____

_____

Waiting on the World to Change

At its best, postmillennialism is a perspective on the end times that highlights the power of the gospel. The postmillennial position emphasizes the capacity of the gospel to transform not only individuals, but also entire communities, cultures—even the world. According to postmillennialists, there will come a time when worldwide acceptance of the gospel ushers in the millennial kingdom. Jesus will not be physically present on earth during this millennium. Instead, Jesus will reign spiritually through the power and proclamation of the gospel.

Nearly everyone throughout the world will trust in Jesus during this time. At some point after the vast majority of Gentiles turn to Jesus, the Jewish people in particular will recognize Jesus as their long-awaited Messiah (Romans 11:13–25). Entire countries and civilizations will change as citizens and leaders alike embrace the good news of Jesus. Satan will be restrained, war will give way to peace, and the saints of God will rule the nations (Revelation 20:2–6).

The first resurrection in Revelation 20:5 is not a physical restoration from the dead, according to postmillennialists; it is the spiritual regeneration that occurs in the life of every follower of Jesus (Ephesians 2:6).

Jesus himself declared that the kingdom was like a seed growing into a tree and like yeast permeating dough (Matthew 13:31–33). What this suggests to postmillennialists is that the millennial kingdom will emerge slowly and then expand to fill the entire world. At the end of this glorious time period, God will allow Satan to deceive the nations for a very brief time (Revelation 20:7–9). In that moment when the Satan-inspired armies of the earth have arrayed themselves against the reign of God, Jesus will return to earth to defeat Satan once and for all (Revelation 20:10–15). Some postmillennialists understand this glorious time period still to be in the future. Others, similar to amillennialists, take the millennium to be a present reality. These postmillennialists place the dawning of the millennial kingdom in the first century AD—perhaps around AD 30 at the ascension of Jesus, or in AD 70 with the destruction of the Jewish temple. This perspective expects a continual expansion of the gospel throughout this time period, until the spiritual reign of Jesus through the gospel fills the entire earth. Kenneth Gentry puts it this way in his book *He Shall Have Dominion*: "Postmillennialism expects that eventually the vast majority of men living will be saved. Increasing gospel success will gradually produce a time in history prior to Christ's return in which faith, righteousness, peace, and prosperity will prevail in the affairs of men and of nations. After an extensive era of such conditions the Lord will return visibly, bodily, and gloriously, to end history with the general resurrection and the final judgment after which the eternal order follows."

- Study Matthew 13:31–33 and Revelation 20:1–15. Explain how a postmillennialist might interpret each of these Scriptures:

  Matthew 13:31–33 _____

  _____

  _____

  Revelation 20:1–15_____

  _____

  _____

- List three ways in which a postmillennial view of the end times might produce God-honoring attitudes or actions in a person's life.

  1. _____

  2. _____

  3. _____

Postmillennialism and Amillennialism: Is There Really Any Difference?

At this point, at least a few of you may be thinking, "Spiritual millennium? And Jesus returns to earth after the millennial kingdom? Isn't that the same as amillennialism?" If that's what you're thinking, you're partly correct: Postmillennialism is similar to amillennialism. In fact, prior to the eighteenth century, Christian theologians didn't consistently distinguish between amillennialism and postmillennialism. That's why you might see—for example—Martin Luther, John Calvin, and sometimes even Augustine identified as amillennialists in one place and as postmillennialists somewhere else!

Here's why the two perspectives are sometimes confused: Both in amillennialism and in postmillennialism, the millennial kingdom is a spiritual reign instead of a physical reign. Also in both perspectives, Jesus returns at the end of the millennium rather than at the beginning. Even with these similarities, however, amillennialism and postmillennialism are far from identical!

Here are two key differences between these two views of the end times:

1. According to amillennialists, the millennial kingdom and the great tribulation occur at the same time. Postmillennialists believe that the millennium takes place after the great tribulation.

2. What's more, according to most amillennialists, Jesus is reigning spiritually with the saints in heaven whereas postmillennialists believe that Jesus will reign spiritually through the gospel on earth.

- What is one similarity between amillennialism and postmillennialism?

  _____

  _____

- What is one difference between amillennialism and postmillennialism?

  _____

  _____

- What is one question that you still have about postmillennialism?

  _____

  _____

Where Did Postmillennialism Come from Anyway?

Hints of postmillennialism can be found in a few writings from ancient and medieval times. For example, fourth-century Christian theologians Eusebius of Caesarea and Athanasius of Alexandria may have been postmillennialists. A twelfth-century monk named Joachim of Fiore expected an "Age of the Holy Spirit"—his term for the millennial kingdom—to begin around 1260.

The forms of postmillennialism that are familiar today, however, can be traced back to the biblical studies of eighteenth-century English theologian Daniel Whitby. As he read Scripture, Whitby became convinced that a time would come when the entire world would turn to Jesus, the Jews would return to the Holy Land, and Muslim nations would be defeated. All of this would mark the beginning of a thousand years of peace, righteousness, and happiness. Jesus would not, however, return physically until this time came to a close.

Around the time that a series of revivals broke out in the American colonies, Whitby's postmillennial views caught the attention of a pastor in Northampton, Massachusetts. These revivals would become known among later generations as the Great Awakening. And what was the Massachusetts pastor's name? It was Jonathan Edwards. He understood these revivals in the Great Awakening as God's preparation of his people for the millennial kingdom. Edwards eagerly anticipated the "future promised advancement of the kingdom of Christ" during the millennium as "an event unspeakably happy and glorious.... It is represented as a time of vast increase of knowledge and understanding ... a time wherein religion and true Christianity shall in every respect be uppermost ... a time wherein vital piety shall take possession of thrones and palaces, and those that are in most exalted stations shall be eminent in holiness ... a time of wonderful union ... wherein the nations shall beat their swords into ploughshares ... and God will cause, wars to cease to the ends of the earth (Isaiah 2; 32–33) … a time wherein all heresies and false doctrines shall be exploded, and the church of God shall not be rent with a variety of jarring opinions … a time wherein the whole earth shall be united as one holy city, one heavenly family." (J. Edwards, *The Works of President Edwards in Eight Volumes*, vol. 3, ed. S. Austin; Isaiah Thomas, 1808; pp. 373–375)

How Much of the End Has Already Passed? A Look at Preterist Postmillennialism

From a postmillennialist perspective, the outlook for the future is bright! As the gospel penetrates the world, every civilization and culture will grow in goodness. Once the millennial kingdom is underway, wars will fade into a distant memory; diseases will be destroyed; and, all humanity will live long and prosper.

But what about the great tribulation? Where can this time of suffering and trials fit into such an optimistic view of the end times? And who might the beast and the antichrist be? Postmillennialists do understand the great tribulation as an event that happens before the millennial kingdom—but postmillennialists differ on exactly when and how the tribulation takes place. Jonathan Edwards, for example, speculated that 1,260 days in Revelation 12:6 might symbolize 1,260 years from the time when the bishop of the city of Rome began to dominate the church. And so, according to Edwards, the years of the great tribulation "began in the year 606, when the pope was first seated in his chair and was made universal bishop. They will therefore, end about 1866." (Quoted in B. Withrow, "A Future of Hope," *Trinity Journal*; Spring 2001, pp. 75–98)

There's another postmillennial perspective on the great tribulation that's become increasingly popular over the past several years: This perspective is known as preterism [PREH-terr-izm]. The word preterism comes from the Latin *praeteritus* ("past" or "bygone") and suggests that many events described in end-times texts happened in the first-century. Theologian R.C. Sproul is probably the best-known orthodox preterist postmillennialist.

₵ Look up and read Matthew 24:1–3

It was around the year AD 30 when Jesus spoke these words. It's clear that he was prophesying about a future event—but what future event was he predicting? Many Christians have understood these words of Jesus as a reference to a great tribulation that, even for us today, remains in the future. Preterists place the fulfillment of this prophecy in a very different time and place, however. According to preterists, this text was fulfilled around the year AD 70. Specifically, preterists point out how Jesus states twice in this text that these afflictions will occur in "this generation" (Matthew 23:36; 24:34)—and the approximate span of a generation in Scripture is forty years (see for example Numbers 14:34).

With that in mind, let's take a look at this text from a preterist perspective and see what we find! What were the disciples actually asking? The disciples asked two questions: (1) When will the Jewish temple be destroyed? And, (2) what will be the sign of the Messiah's "return" and "the end of the age"? In preterist perspective, the Messiah's return does not refer to the physical return of Jesus to earth; it refers instead to his judgment of the nation of Israel because they rejected Jesus as their Messiah. "The end of the age" points to the ending of a chapter in God's work with the nation of Israel. According to preterists, the destruction of Jerusalem in AD 70 answered both of the disciples' questions.

ℭ Look up and read Matthew 24:4–28

When was the time of false messiahs? Matthew 24:4–14: "Many will come in my name, saying 'I am the Christ'" Jesus predicted in these verses, and that's precisely what occurred in the years approaching AD 70—as did earthquakes and conflicts and famines! An earthquake rocked Pompeii in AD 62. The Jewish historian Josephus described the 50s and 60s as a time when "the country was filled anew with robbers and impostors.... These impostors and deceivers persuaded the multitude to follow them into the desert, and pretended that they would exhibit manifest wonders and signs, that should be performed by the providence of God." (Josephus, *Antiquitates Judaicae*, 20:8:5–6)

Then, of course, there was the war that broke out in AD 66 between several bands of Jewish revolutionaries and the Romans. At first, there were Jewish victories, including an ambush at Beth-Horon that resulted in the slaughter of an entire Roman legion. By the late 60s, revolts were blazing not only among the Jews in Judea and Galilee but also among other people-groups in Gaul, Spain, and Africa. In AD 68, Emperor Nero committed suicide and—before Vespasian rose to the rank of emperor in AD 69—three other emperors rose and fell amid vicious conflicts in Rome. Under Vespasian and later his son

Titus, more Roman legions arrived in Galilee and Judea, sweeping southward toward Jerusalem and crushing every hint of rebellion. On the shores of the Sea of Galilee, Josephus wrote, "one could see the whole lake red with blood and covered with corpses, for not a man escaped." (Josephus, *Bellum Judaicum*, 3:10:9). During the siege of Jerusalem, food was so scarce in the city that a woman cooked her own infant, ate half of the body, and offered the other half to others.

But had the gospel been proclaimed in "the whole world" by this time, as Jesus predicted in Matthew 24:14? The phrase "the whole world" may simply mean that the gospel has been made available beyond the Jewish people, to people of every nation. And, according to Paul, when he wrote his letter to the Colossians around AD 57, the gospel had reached "the whole world" (Colossians 1:5–6; see also Romans 1:8). So—according to preterists—everything that Jesus described in these verses found its fulfillment in the years leading up to the destruction of the Jewish temple.

What was the "abomination of desolations"? (Matthew 24:15–28). The prophet Daniel predicted a day when "the people of the prince who is to come shall destroy the city and the sanctuary.... On the wing of abominations shall come one who makes desolate" (Daniel 9:26–27). Many biblical scholars—not only among postmillennialists but also among amillennialists and historical premillennialists—see the Roman army's entrance into the Jewish temple in AD 70 as a fulfillment of Daniel's prophecy. Ancient church leaders such as Athanasius of Alexandria, Augustine of Hippo, and John Chrysostom also understood this desecration of the temple to be the abomination of desolations.

And indeed, in those horrible moments when the Romans swept through the city of Jerusalem, the Jewish temple was desolated in the most abominable ways. According to Jewish tradition, Titus—the general of the Roman army—dragged a harlot into the Holy of Holies and committed fornication with her there on top of a scroll that contained the Hebrew Scriptures. (For rabbinic references to this event, see *Anthony Saldarini*, trans., Abot de Rabbi Nathan; Brill, 1975; pp. 67–69).

Roman soldiers carried their battle standards into the temple courts. Atop every standard was the image of an eagle, a creature that the soldiers worshiped. Significantly, the Greek word translated vulture in Matthew 24:28 also means eagle. Could it be that Jesus prophetically glimpsed these idolatrous Roman battle standards forty years before the Romans set foot in the temple courts?

- Carefully read Matthew 24:1–28 in at least two different translations of the Bible. Review the historical backgrounds above. Based on what you understand now, which portions of this passage might have been fulfilled in the first century?

_____

_____

_____

ℭ Look up and read Matthew 24:29–31

It's at this point that other perspectives part ways with preterism. After all, how could this text have possibly been fulfilled in the first century? If "the Son of Man [came] on the clouds of heaven with power and great glory," wouldn't everyone have noticed? Doesn't this passage describe the end of all time?

Not necessarily! At least in the preterist perspective, Jesus may have been referring to something very different than the end of time. In the first place, many of the terms in this text draw from Old Testament images of divine reckoning or judgment. Remember how Isaiah described the fall of Babylon that occurred in 539 BC? "The stars ... will not give their light. The sun will be dark at rising, and the moon will not give its light" (Isaiah 13:10). Ezekiel used similar language to depict the fall of Egypt (Ezekiel 32:7–8). The prophet Isaiah even reported a vision of God coming on the clouds of heaven to judge Egypt (Isaiah 19:1).

Did God physically ride on a cloud over the continent of Africa when Egypt fell? Probably not. Were the sun and moon darkened once and for all when the nations of Babylon and Egypt fell? Of course not! These declarations were prophetic descriptions of God's judgment on specific nations. In the same way—preterists suggest—Jesus drew from the language of these prophets to describe God's judgment on Israel in AD 70. And, as for the "loud trumpet call," this too could depict a time of divine reckoning in the Old Testament prophets (Isaiah 27:13; 58:1; Jeremiah 4:5–21; Hosea 8:1).

But what about "the sign of the Son of Man"? According to Matthew 24:30, "the tribes"—possibly a reference to the tribes of Israel—"will see the Son of Man coming on the clouds!" Could such an event really have happened in the first century? In response, preterists point out that not only Jewish people, but also Romans did report unexpected happenings in the clouds around AD 70:

Josephus, Jewish historian: "I suppose this account would seem to be false except that eyewitnesses vouched for it: ... Before sunset, chariots were seen in the air over the whole land, and armored soldiers were speeding through the clouds and encircling the cities. ... As the priests were going by night into the inner court, they felt a quaking and heard a great noise. After that, they heard a sound something like a large crowd saying, 'Let us leave this place.'" (Josephus, *Bellum Judaicum*, 6:5:3)

Tacitus, Roman historian: "In the sky, there appeared a vision of armies in glittering armor in conflict. Then a lightning flash from the clouds illuminated the temple! The doors of this holy place suddenly opened, a superhuman voice was heard declaring that the gods were leaving, and at the same time came the sound of a rushing tumult." (Tacitus, *Annales*, 5:13)

In light of these reports, is it possible that some "sign of the Son of Man" did appear in the skies around AD 70? Many orthodox preterists think so. If the preterists are correct on this point, it could be that the great tribulation (Matthew 24:21) occurred in those ghastly years between the beginning of the Jewish-Roman War in AD 66 and the fall of Jerusalem in 70. After Jerusalem fell, God began to "gather his elect" from among the Gentiles (Matthew 24:31); this will continue until the "fullness of the Gentiles" comes to faith in Jesus (Romans 11:25).

- Carefully read Matthew 24:29–31 in at least two different translations of the Bible. Review the historical backgrounds above. Based on what you understand now, which portions of this passage might have been fulfilled in the first century?

_____

_____

_____

- Earlier, you wrote one question that you had about postmillennialism. Did you discover an answer to that question during this study? If so, write the answer in the space below.

_____

_____

_____

666

The content of the mark of the beast will be "the name of the beast or the number of his name" and this number is "six hundred and sixty-six" (Revelation 13:18). But what was the meaning of this beastly number? No one knows for certain, but here are some facts that may help your understanding: In some ancient languages, letters also functioned as numbers. The first letter of the alphabet might mean "one," while the second would mean "two." The eleventh letter might imply 20, the twelfth letter 30, and so on. It was possible to add letters and come up with the number of someone's name. An example of how this process functioned can be found in the first-century ruins of Pompeii. There, archaeologists have unearthed a fragment of graffiti that reads, "I love her whose number is 545." Another example of this process can be found in a document known as the Sibylline Oracles, where the number of Jesus' name is calculated as 888.

With this background in mind, there are a couple of possible meanings for 666, both of which could be true. It's possible that John knew how Jesus' name added up to 888—each digit moving one beyond seven, a number that the Jews identified with completeness. By connecting 666 with the beast—each digit of 666 falling one short of seven—John predicted a world ruler who would fall short of God's glory in every way. The other possibility emphasizes how the name of Emperor Nero adds up to 666 when written in Hebrew letters. If the character of Nero was what John had in mind, the inspired author may have been referring to a world ruler who, like Nero, persecutes God's people. Since Nero was the sixth emperor from Julius Caesar, some interpreters also suggest that Nero was the sixth king in Revelation 17:10 and that Revelation was written during Nero's reign. (For more on the mark of the beast, see B. Witherington III, *Revelation*; Cambridge University Press, 2003; pp. 184–185)

Never Underestimate the Power of the Light

Of course, orthodox preterists—as well as other postmillennialists—also believe that Jesus will someday return physically to earth. When that time comes, "the dead in Christ will rise first. Then we who are alive, who are left, will be caught up together with them in the clouds to meet the Lord in the air" (1 Thessalonians 4:17–18; see also Acts 1:9–11; 1 Corinthians 15:51–52). According to postmillennialists, this will occur after a long period of earthly peace. In the meantime, if you are a postmillennialist, your task is to proclaim the gospel to all people in preparation for the dawning of a millennial kingdom!

And what if you're not a postmillennialist? Perhaps you've concluded that postmillennialism and preterism fall far short in their interpretations of Scripture. If that's the case, don't despair! You can still learn from both of these perspectives. Even if you don't believe that the destruction of the temple in AD 70 fulfilled the prophecies of Jesus in Matthew 24, preterism is a reminder of how important that event was to people in the first century. And, when it comes to postmillennialism, the emphasis on the power of the gospel should call every Christian to be more passionate about proclaiming how the gospel can transform people's lives.

Regardless of your millennial perspective, it is possible to embrace the belief that the gospel really can change the world. And, by gospel, I mean far more than the initial statement that helps someone understand how to confess Jesus as the risen Lord—although such statements are certainly important! What I also mean is the constant awareness that, in every moment of my life, I desperately need what God has provided in the crucified Christ. The gospel is my constant reminder that any good that I may do is only because of grace that God has lavished on me in Jesus Christ. Whatever problem I may face in life, the gospel forms the foundation for God's solution—and, if the gospel is not foundational to the solution, either I don't understand the problem or I don't understand the gospel. That's the true power of the gospel. And, even if you're not a postmillennialist, that's good news.

> *Never underestimate the power of the gospel! Postmillennialism emphasizes the power of the gospel to transform not only individuals but also communities, cultures, and the world.*

Now What?

PRAY: Heavenly Father, work in me so that I may see your gospel as good news not only for the dead but also for the living, not only for the sick but also for the whole, not only for the lost but also for the found. Through the same Holy Spirit who breathed new life into the flesh of your Blessed Son, breathe new life into my passion for your holy gospel. I yield this prayer to the holy name of Jesus. Amen.

LEARN: Study chapters 8, 9, 10, 11, 12, and 13 in the book of Revelation. Consider carefully which—if any—of the prophecies found in these chapters could have been fulfilled in AD 70. Memorize Revelation 11:15–18.

Do: What person, in your daily life, do you perceive to be beyond the reach of God's grace? Never underestimate the power of the gospel! Develop a deliberate and specific plan for the upcoming month to work toward living and speaking the gospel in that person's life.

Rapture Ready?
Dispensational Premillennialism

Get This:

Always be ready for the return of Jesus.

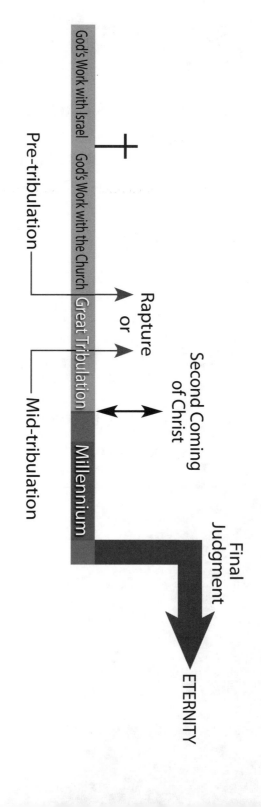

Dispensational Premillennialism

God's Work with Israel
God's Work with the Church
Pre-tribulation
Great Tribulation
Rapture
or
Mid-tribulation
Millennium
Rapture
Second Coming
of Christ
Final
Judgment
ETERNITY

Session 5 Outline
Rapture Ready? Dispensational Premillennialism

1. Dispensational Premillennialism

    a. Jesus will remove the church before a 7-year tribulation

    b. 144,000 and the great multitude

        49 yrs.

        27 A.D.

2. Dispensations

    a. Hebrew people, Genesis 15:18

    b. The Church Age

3. Seven years of tribulation

    a. God renews his work with Israel

    b. Temple will be rebuilt

    c. Land will be received by Israel

    d. Jews will turn to Jesus

    e. One world government, religion

    f. War, persecution, disasters, Daniel 9:27

      g. A world leader

      h. God removes the church before this tribulation, 1 Thessalonians 5:9

4.   History of Dispensationalism

      a. Pseudo-Ephraem the Syrian

      b. John Nelson Darby, 19th century

      c. Scofield Reference Bible

      d. Hal Lindsey, Tim LaHaye

5.   The Dispensational Premillennial perspective

      a. Historical grammatical approach

      b. Literal 1,000 years, Revelation 20:4–6

6.   Strengths of Dispensational Premillennialism

      a. Takes Scripture seriously

      b. Extremely passionate about evangelism

      c. Expectant about the return of Jesus, Mark 13:33–37

Key Terms

144,000 Jewish believers in Jesus, designated by God to proclaim the gospel during the great tribulation (Revelation 7:1–8). Through their testimony, a great multitude from every nation will trust Jesus during the great tribulation (Revelation 7:9–17).

Apocalypse of Pseudo-Ephraem the Syrian Seventh-century Syrian text, falsely written under Ephraem's name nearly 300 years after Ephraem died. The text describes the rise of Islam in apocalyptic terms.

Dispensation A distinguishable outworking of a divine plan with a particular people; a period of time during which humanity is tested in respect of obedience to some specific revelation of the will of God.

Dispensational Premillennialism God will rapture Christians from the world before the great tribulation. Jesus will return to earth after the seven-year great tribulation, before ("pre-") the millennium described in Revelation 20.

Great Multitude The people who trust in Jesus Christ during the great tribulation.

Historical Grammatical Approach The method of interpretation that attempts to determine the author's original intended meaning in a text. Some dispensational premillennialists understand this approach to require interpreters to take every aspect of a text literally, regardless of literary genre, unless a literal interpretation is somehow impossible.

John Nelson Darby (1800–1882) English-Irish Bible teacher and evangelist, credited with developing and popularizing dispensationalism. Darby never formally studied theology or biblical literature; he was trained as a lawyer before becoming an Anglican clergyman.

Mark of the beast According to Revelation, a time will come when everyone is compelled "to be marked on the right hand or forehead" (Revelation 13:16). Some Bible teachers understand this to be some sort of physical implant or mark. Other interpreters point out how, in the Old Testament, God commanded his people to place the memory of their redemption "as a mark on your hand, even bound between your eyes" (Exodus 13:16). In the same way, a mark "on the right hand or forehead" could simply imply acting and thinking in accordance with this beast.

Rapture (from Latin *raptus*, "catching up") The meeting of Jesus and his people in the air, described in 1 Thessalonians 4:13–18. Nearly all dispensational premillennialists understand the rapture as an event that will occur before the great tribulation (pre-tribulation). A few dispensationalists treat the rapture as an event that happens during the great tribulation (mid-tribulation). Every view of the end times except dispensational premillennialism views the rapture and the return of Jesus as two parts of same event. Dispensational premillennialists understand the rapture and return as two separate events.

Seven-year Tribulation The "seventieth week" described in Daniel 9:24, when God will continue his work with the earthly nation of Israel and pour out his wrath throughout the earth.

Caught Up in the End Times

Chances are, you're already familiar with dispensational premillennialism—even if you've never heard the phrase before! Have you ever read a novel with the title *Left Behind* embossed on the cover? Or how about one of the bestselling books of the twentieth century, *The Late, Great Planet Earth*? Maybe you've used a *Scofield Reference Bible* or a *Ryrie Study Bible* at some point. Perhaps you've even watched a movie with a title like *A Thief in the Night* or *Prodigal Planet*.

If any of these possibilities rings a bell in your mind, you know at least a little bit about dispensational premillennialism. In some churches, dispensationalism has dominated discussions of the end times since the early twelfth century. As a result, many contemporary Christians have never even heard about any view of the end times other than dispensational premillennialism. And yet, simply because dispensational ideas are so widespread doesn't mean that they shouldn't be studied! Sometimes what we know the best is what we need to study the most. With that in mind, let's take a look at what will transpire in the end times from the perspective of dispensational premillennialism.

♫ Look up and read 1 Thessalonians 4:15–5:9

Paul's visit to the city of Thessalonica hadn't gone particularly well (see Asia Minor map). Soon after Paul and Silas began teaching in the city, a riot forced them to flee—perhaps less than a month after they arrived! (Acts 17:2–10). As a result, Paul may not have had opportunity to teach the Thessalonians adequately. Shortly after leaving Thessalonica, Paul sent his trusted coworker Timothy to check on these new believers. Most of what Timothy discovered was encouraging (1 Thessalonians 3:6), but there were some serious doctrinal difficulties brewing beneath the surface. Misguided teachers were claiming that Jesus had already returned. The Thessalonian Christians feared that they and their deceased loved ones had somehow missed this momentous event! Of course, they had no reason to fear, because the second coming of Jesus was yet to come. And that's why Paul wrote the letter that's been titled "The First

Epistle of Paul to the Thessalonians" in your New Testament—to reassure the Thessalonian church regarding the return of Jesus. Paul made it clear to the Thessalonians that, whenever Jesus returned, no Christian could possibly miss this event! Jesus would descend "with a cry of command, with the voice of an archangel, and with the sound of the trumpet of God" (4:16). At this moment, deceased Christians will be resurrected, followed immediately by living believers. The precise timing of this event will be unpredictable—"like a thief in the night," Paul predicted—but, for Christians, it will be impossible to overlook (5:2).

Thus far, every orthodox view of the end-times—amillennialism, postmillennialism, both forms of premillennialism, and even orthodox preterism—would agree: Someday, Jesus will return and his people will be caught up to meet him in the air. This event is also known as the rapture. Despite some claims to the contrary, *rapture* is a biblical term. In the Latin version of 1 Thessalonians 4:17, the word translated "caught up" in English versions is rendered by the verb *rapiemur* from the noun *raptus*. The English word *rapture* comes from the Latin *raptus* and simply means "being caught up."

Here's where dispensational premillennialism begins to diverge from other perspectives on the end times: Every end-times viewpoint except dispensational premillennialism sees the rapture of the church and the return of Jesus to earth as two parts of one single event. Dispensational premillennialism, however, treats the rapture and the return as two separate events in God's plan.

ℭ The Rapture and Jesus' Return as Separate Events in Dispensational Premillennialism

Rapture of the Church	Jesus' Return to Earth
The rapture will occur at an unexpected time (1 Thessalonians 5:2; Matthew 24:44).	Jesus will return to earth after a seven-year great tribulation (Matthew 24:29).
Jesus will return for his church (1 Thessalonians 4:13–18).	Jesus will return with his church (Revelation 19:14).
Believers will be taken into God the Father's presence (John 14:3).	Believers will come to earth (Matthew 24:30).
Only believers will experience the rapture (1 Corinthians 15:52).	Every eye will see Jesus as the returning king (Matthew 24:30; Revelation 1:7; 19:11–16).
No battle with Satan is mentioned in connection with the rapture.	Satan is bound (Revelation 20:1–3).
No judgment of the earth is mentioned in connection with the rapture.	The earth is judged (Revelation 20:4–5).
The rapture is a mystery (1 Corinthians 15:51).	The return of Jesus was foretold in the Old Testament (Daniel 12:1–3; Zechariah 12:10; 14:4).

• What does the word "rapture" mean?

_____

• Carefully study each Scripture in the chart. Review what you learned about Matthew 24 in the session on postmillennialism and preterism. Write three questions that you have about dispensational premillennialism?

1. _____

2. _____

3. _____

Dispensational premillennialists understand Revelation 4:1–2 as a reference to the rapture and Revelation 19:1–20:3 as a description of the glorious return of

Jesus to earth. Other views of the end times do not take Revelation 4:1–2 as a description of the rapture. Views other than dispensational premillennialism see both rapture and return in Revelation 19:1–20:3. According to these perspectives, the church is caught up to meet Jesus (1 Thessalonians 4:13–18; Revelation 19:7–9) and then immediately to return to earth as part of his royal retinue (Revelation 19:14).

- Study Revelation 4:1–2 and Revelation 19:11–20:3. Based on your present understanding, do the rapture and the return of Jesus seem to you more like two separate events or like two parts of the same event? Why?

_____

_____

_____

Two Purposes, Two Peoples

The separation of the rapture from the glorious return is not, however, the only distinguishing mark of dispensational premillennialism. In fact, this division of rapture and return is the result of a much deeper and more substantive distinction. The most important difference between dispensational premillennialism and other viewpoints has to do with how dispensationalists separate God's work with Israel from God's work with the church. Of course, every view of the end times recognizes some distinction between Israel and the church—but other viewpoints treat God's work with the nation of Israel as preparation for the coming of Jesus and for the fulfillment of God's promises through the church. For dispensational premillennialists, however, God's work with Israel was not merely preparatory; God has two separate plans with two separate peoples, the church and the nation of Israel. According to Lewis Sperry Chafer, "The dispensationalist believes that throughout the ages God is pursuing two distinct purposes: one related to the earth with earthly people and earthly objectives involved, which is Judaism; while the other is related to heaven with heavenly people and heavenly objectives involved, which is Christianity." (L.S. Chafer, *Dispensationalism*; Dallas Theological Seminary, 1995; p. 107)

> *This distinction between Israel and the church is "the most basic theological test of whether or not a person is a dispensationalist, and it is undoubtedly the most practical and conclusive."*
> (C.C. Ryrie, Dispensationalism; Moody, 2007; p. 46)

- Summarize, in your own words, what is most distinctive about dispensationalism:

_____

_____

_____

ℭ *Views on Israel and the Church*

	The Nation of Israel	**The Church**
Dispensational Premillennialism	God has purposed to work with two different groups of people—Israel and the church—in different dispensations. God will fulfill his promises to the patriarchs and to the Jewish people through the modern nation of Israel.	The church is a spiritual work separate from God's earthly work with the political nation of Israel. During the great tribulation, God will remove the church from the world and continue his work with the nation of Israel.
Amillennialism, Postmillennialism, and Historical premillennialism	God has always had one plan and one people. God's work with the nation of Israel was preparatory for his revelation of himself through Jesus and for his work with the church. Before the end of time, a great spiritual awakening will bring many Jewish people to faith in Jesus as their Messiah.	It is through Jesus and through the church that God is fulfilling the promises that he made to the patriarchs and to the people of Israel. In the Old Testament and the New, God's purpose has always been to redeem every person who would trust in the Messiah. Jesus came to accomplish this redemption through his death and resurrection.

How Do I Get a Dispensation?

God's work with Israel and with the church represent two different dispensations—that's where the term dispensational comes from. Premillennial comes from the belief that Jesus will return to earth before (pre-) the millennial kingdom; Jesus will reign physically on earth during the millennium.

And what is a dispensation? Here's a simple definition of dispensation: It's a distinguishable outworking of a divine plan with a particular people. In each dispensation, God governs the world differently and places different responsibilities on humanity. Every dispensationalist recognizes at least two dispensations: (1) a dispensation of Law in the Old Testament, and (2) a dispensation of grace in the New Testament. Most dispensationalists also recognize some sort of distinguishable divine work with the patriarchs, before Moses received the Law, and during the millennial kingdom when God both fulfills his promises to Israel and blesses people from all nations.

And how does all of this influence the dispensational distinction between rapture and return?

1. In the rapture, God removes the church from the world so that he can resume or continue his work with the earthly nation of Israel. In Genesis 15:18, God promised to the seed of Abraham all the land from the Nile River to the Euphrates River. According to dispensational premillennialists, the earthly nation of Israel—the physical descendants of Abraham—must someday rule this land. Dispensationalists see the establishment of the modern state of Israel in 1948 as a crucial part of the prophetic puzzle that will culminate in the Israelis controlling not only Palestine but also every piece of land from Egypt to Iraq.

2. This desire to renew his work with Israel isn't the only reason why God must remove the church from the world, however! It's also because the great tribulation will be a time when divine wrath will be experienced throughout the earth. According to the apostle Paul, believers in Jesus Christ are "not destined ... for wrath, but to obtain salvation through our Lord Jesus Christ" (1 Thessalonians 5:9). Dispensational premillennialists take this verse to mean that God will remove Christians from the world before he unleashes his wrath during the great tribulation.

• Why do dispensational premillennialists believe that God will remove the church from the world before the great tribulation?

_____

_____

_____

How Many Dispensations?

Even though dispensationalists may differ on the precise number of dispensations, all dispensational premillennialists agree that God has worked in particular and distinguishable ways with different groups of people throughout history.

Dispensational theologian John Nelson Darby suggested six dispensations:

Dispensation of Noah From the covenant with Noah until the calling of Abraham
Dispensation of Abraham From the calling of Abraham until the Law of Moses
Dispensation of Israel (Law, Priesthood, and Kings) From Law of Moses to Exile, resumed with Daniel's seventieth week during the great tribulation
Dispensation of the Gentiles From the exile of Judah until the coming of Jesus
Dispensation of the Church From the establishment of the church until the rapture
Millennial Kingdom After the great tribulation

"And he shall make a strong covenant with many for one week, and for half of the week he shall put an end to sacrifice and offering. And on the wing of abominations shall come one who makes desolate, until the decreed end is poured out on the desolator."—*Daniel 9:27 ESV*

Here's what many dispensational premillennialists expect to happen near the time of the rapture: Many nations—described in the prophecies of Ezekiel as Gog and Magog, Meshech and Tubal—will rise against the modern state of Israel (Ezekiel 38–39). The Israelis will respond by signing a treaty with a world leader who is the Beast and the Antichrist (Revelation 11:7; 13:1–8; 1 John 2:18). This treaty is, from the perspective of dispensational premillennialists, the "strong covenant" revealed here to the prophet Daniel. The Antichrist will assist in the rebuilding of a new Jewish temple in Jerusalem. Sacrifices and offerings will resume.

The ratification of the "strong covenant" will mark the beginning of the great tribulation. Before this final seven years begins, God will rapture his church and resume his work with the earthly nation of Israel. These seven years of the great tribulation are known prophetically as Daniel's "seventieth week" (Daniel 9:24). According to dispensational premillennialists, these seven years at the end of time were what John saw and described beginning in Revelation 4 and continuing through Revelation 19.

Near the beginning of the great tribulation, God will designate 144,000 Jewish believers in Jesus to proclaim the gospel during this time of trouble (Revelation 7:1–8). Through their testimony, a great multitude from every nation will trust Jesus during the great tribulation (Revelation 7:9–17).

Halfway through the great tribulation, the Antichrist will break his treaty with the Israelis and desecrate the very temple that he helped to build. In the words of the prophet Daniel, "he shall put an end to sacrifice and offering" (Daniel 9:27). The wrath of God will be unleashed on the earth like never before (Revelation 16). In the end, the armies of the earth will array themselves against God's people. When all hope will seem to have failed, the King of kings and Lord of lords will return to earth and defeat his enemies with the mere words of his mouth (Revelation 19). For one thousand years, Jesus will reign from Jerusalem, and Satan will be bound. At the end of this peaceful millennium, Satan will be released, defeated, and—along with every enemy of the living God—forever consigned to the lake of fire (Revelation 20:7–15).

The Temple in Revelation

In Revelation 11:1–2, John measures the temple. Here are four possible understandings: (1) Dispensational premillennialists and some historical premillennialists take the temple to be a new Jewish temple that will be physically constructed during the great tribulation or perhaps during the millennial kingdom. (2) Others see the measuring as a symbol of how, even though the powers of this world besiege the church, God still preserves his church. (3) Still others understand the measuring as a symbol of how God is preserving the Jewish people in preparation for a great spiritual awakening before Jesus returns (Romans 11:5–32). (4) Some preterist postmillennialists take the measuring of the temple not as setting aside a place for preservation but as designating the Jewish temple for destruction—a designation that was fulfilled with the Romans' destruction of this temple in AD 70.

- Study Daniel 9:24–27 and Revelation 7:1–17. Review what you have learned about amillennialism and postmillennialism.

How Dispensationalism Grew

Dispensational premillennialism is a relatively recent view of the end times. In fact, the earliest hint in church history of a pre-tribulation rapture is found in an obscure Latin text known as Apocalypse of Pseudo-Ephraem. According to this text, "All the saints and elect of God are gathered before the tribulation, which is to come, and are taken to the Lord." There are, however, difficulties with reading very much into this text. In the first place, this text wasn't written by the fourth-century theologian Ephraem at all. It was falsely written in Ephraem's name nearly 300 years after his death. That's why the document is attributed to pseudo-Ephraem. Furthermore, the text was originally written in Greek, but this line appears only in a Latin translation from the eighth or ninth centuries. (For texts of pseudo-Ephraem, see E. Beck, ed., *Des heiligen Ephraem des Syrers Sermones III, Louvain: Secrétariat du Corpus*, 197; pp. 60-71. T. Lamy, ed., *Sancti Ephraem Syri Hymni et Sermones* vol. 3; *Mechliniae: Dessain*, 1897; pp. 187–212)

In 1744, a ministry student named Morgan Edwards speculated in a term paper that Christians might be removed from the world during or before the great tribulation. It wasn't until 1833, however, that anyone publicly proclaimed the form of dispensationalism that is so familiar today. That individual was John Nelson Darby, who described the church age as "a great parenthesis of prophetic time" between 69th and 70th weeks of the prophet Daniel. Throughout the mid-nineteenth century, Darby developed a dispensational system that separated God's work with Israel from God's work with the church.

During this era, the influences of American transcendentalism and German higher criticism were pressing seminaries throughout North America in the direction of theological liberalism. Instead of taking dispensational views to increasingly-liberal seminaries, Darby and others like him proclaimed dispensational premillennialism at Bible conferences and among Bible-believing pastors in large evangelical churches. As a result, by the early twentieth century, dispensational premillennialism became synonymous with taking a stand against theological liberalism in many denominations.

Why Dispensational Premillennialism Matters

Even if you disagree with the dispensational perspective there's much that you can learn from dispensationalism. In the first place, dispensational premillennialists take Scripture seriously. Virtually without exception, dispensationalists believe the Bible to constitute unfailing truth without any mixture of error. That's why teachers like Tim LaHaye declare, "The best guide to Bible study is 'The Golden Rule of Biblical Interpretation': When the plain sense of Scripture makes common sense, seek no other sense, but take every word at its primary, literal meaning unless the facts of the immediate context clearly indicate otherwise." (T. LaHaye, *No Fear of the Storm;* Multnomah, 1992; p. 240)

Dispensationalists want to trust and to obey what the text of Scripture says. Dispensational premillennialism also reminds Christians that God has not forsaken the Jewish people. You may not agree with precisely how dispensationalists understand that God will work with the Jewish people at the end of time—and that's okay! But regardless of your perspective on the end times, dispensational premillennialism serves as a reminder that an anti-Jewish faith is not the faith of Jesus and the apostles. Christian faith and anti-Semitic sentiments are mutually exclusive. Authentic faith in Jesus draws from a rich Hebrew heritage and deeply values the Jewish people. This does not mean that Christians must support every action of the largely secular government of the modern state of Israel. It does mean that Christians must stand with the Jewish people against any and every form of anti-Semitism.

Finally, dispensational premillennialism strongly emphasizes the need to proclaim the gospel now. Christians could be removed from the world at any moment; so, the time to speak the gospel into the lives of people around us is now. "Now is the favorable time; behold, now is the day of salvation" (2 Corinthians 6:2). None of the successes or possessions that surround you at this moment will make it into eternity. But the souls that embrace the truth of Jesus? Those will shine like stars forever and ever (Daniel 12:3).

> *Always be ready for the coming of Jesus. Dispensational premillennialism emphasizes the need for Christians to share the good news of Jesus before it is too late.*

Now What?

PRAY: My Lord and my God, I do not know the time when I will be caught up to meet you. Awaken my heart to long for that moment when you reveal your glory. As I wait, work in me so that I yearn not only for my salvation but also for the salvation of those around me. In the name of the Messiah-King. Amen.

LEARN: Study chapters 14, 15, 16, 17, 18, and 19 in the book of Revelation. As you read these texts, compare and contrast the different approaches that amillennialists, postmillennialists, and dispensational premillennialists would take as they read these Scriptures. Memorize Revelation 19:11–16 or Mark 13:32–33.

DO: Imagine that you will be caught up to meet Jesus in the air one week from today. Make a list of everything you would do this week if you knew for certain that would happen. Across the top of the list, write Mark 13:32–33. Pray through your list. Ask God to show you which items on the list you should undertake in the upcoming week.

Through Tribulation to Everlasting Life: Historical Premillennialism

Get This:

God grows his people through trials and tribulations.

Historical Premillennialism

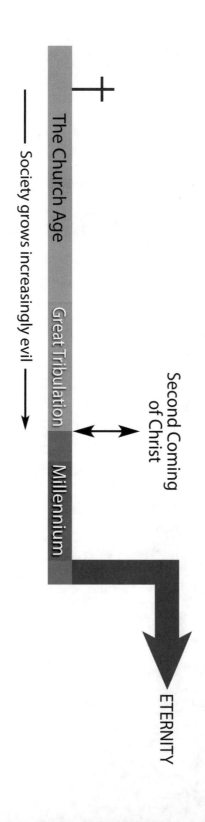

The Church Age

Great Tribulation

Millennium

— Society grows increasingly evil →

Second Coming
of Christ

ETERNITY

Session 6 Outline
Through Tribulation to Everlasting Life:
Historical Premillennialism

1. Historical Premillennialsim

    a. Physical reign of Jesus Christ upon the earth

    b. Church endures the time of tribulation

    c. God has one plan and one people

2. Revelation 7

    a. 144,000; James 1:1; Galatians 6:16; Philippians 3:3

    b. They are sealed during the tribulation

    c. Tribulation is from the beginning of the church to the end

    d. Great multitude is the 144,000; Revelation 5:5−6

3. Why is it called "historical premillennialism"?

    a. Earliest view of the end times

b. Papias

c. Justin Martyr

d. Irenaeus

4. What about Israel?

   a. John measures the temple, Revelation 11:1

   b. God still has plans for Israel, Romans 11:12–15

   c. Two witnesses, Revelation 11:3–4

5. What about the land?

   a. God fulfills his promise in a greater way, Galatians 3:16

6. How do you end a study of the end?

   a. "Come, Lord Jesus," Revelation 20:20

   b. Endure patiently, love others

   c. This life is preparation for a greater life

Key Terms

Great Multitude The church viewed from the viewpoint of eternity, after every tribulation has ended. The church is both the 144,000 sealed in Revelation 7:4 and the great multitude saved in Revelation 7:9—the same people, described from two different perspectives.

Historical Premillennialism After a time of tribulation, Jesus will physically return to earth before the millennial kingdom described in Revelation 20.

Irenaeus of Lyons (AD 130–200) A student of Polycarp, who had been a disciple of the apostle John—wrote that "ten kings shall give their kingdom to the beast and cause the church to flee.... After the antichrist has devastated all things in this world, he will reign for three years and six months." (Irenaeus, *Adversus Haereses*, 5:26:1; 5:30:4)

Justin Martyr (AD 100–165) Christian philosopher who declared, "The man of apostasy, who speaks strange things against the Most High, will venture to do unlawful deeds on the earth against us, the Christians.... I and others—who are right-minded Christians on all points—are assured that there will be a resurrection of the dead, and one thousand years in Jerusalem, which will at that time be built, adorned, and enlarged." (Justin Martyr, *Dialogus cum Tryphoni*, 80, 110)

Papias of Hierapolis (AD 60–130) Received teachings from the apostle John himself. According to Papias, "After the resurrection of the dead, there will be a Millennium, when the personal reign of the Messiah will be established on this earth.... All animals, feeding only on what the earth itself produces, will become peaceable and harmonious, submitting themselves to humanity." (Papias, *Fragments*)

The Battle before the Victory

Heroes of the fictional variety never seem to reach final victory without enduring trials and tribulations. Perhaps you've read C.S. Lewis' classic series *The Chronicles of Narnia*. If so, do you recall the final chapters of *The Last Battle*? Before finding themselves in the everlasting beauty of Aslan's country, those who still believe in Aslan endure intense suffering at the hands of cruel Calormene soldiers.

And it isn't just in Narnia that this principle holds true. It's woven throughout our most familiar films and fairy tales. Before the prince can defeat the sorceress and kiss Sleeping Beauty, he must battle a dragon and a hedge of thorns. Before Dorothy reduces the Wicked Witch to a puddle on the floor, she endures a perilous pilgrimage to Oz, a manic mob of flying monkeys, and imprisonment in the witch's castle. Regardless of what sorts of stories happen to be stacked beside your TV or your bed at this moment, you can find at least a few examples of how final victories require the heroes to endure tribulation.

According to historical premillennialists, it isn't only our fictional storylines that unfold in this way. That's also how God's storyline works. From the perspective of historical premillennialism, the great tribulation is an event that is endured not only by non-believers but also by the church of the Lord Jesus. Throughout the New Testament, the word saints refers to the church (1 Corinthians 1:2; 2 Corinthians 1:1; Ephesians 1:1; 2:19; 4:12; Philippians 1:1; Colossians 1:2–4, 12, 26; Philemon 1:5–7), and—according to the book of Revelation—the saints are still on the earth during the great tribulation (Revelation 13:7–10; 14:12). The saints of God do not reach their final victory by being removed before the great tribulation; instead, they make their way to victory by remaining faithful through the great tribulation.

What's "Historical" about Historical Premillennialism?

Let's first take a look at the title "historical premillennialism." Premillennialism makes sense—that simply means Jesus will return before (pre-) the millennial kingdom to reign physically on the earth. But why is historical premillennialism known as "historical"? The word "historical" appears in the title because, as far as anyone can tell, historical premillennialism was the earliest Christian view of the end times. Historical premillennialism was clearly the predominant perspective on the end of time in the earliest centuries of Christian faith.

Carefully read each of the following quotations from the church leaders who lived soon after the apostles. Consider each one's perspective on the end times:

- Papias of Hierapolis was born in the first century and received teachings from the apostle John himself. According to Papias, "After the resurrection of the dead, there will be a Millennium, when the personal reign of the Messiah will be established on this earth.... All animals, feeding only on what the earth itself produces, will become peaceable and harmonious, submitting themselves to humanity." (Papias, *Fragments*)

- In the mid-second century, a Christian philosopher named Justin declared, "The man of apostasy, who speaks strange things against the Most High, will venture to do unlawful deeds on the earth against us, the Christians.... I and others—who are right-minded Christians on all points—are assured that there will be a resurrection of the dead, and one thousand years in Jerusalem, which will at that time be built, adorned, and enlarged." (Justin Martyr, *Dialogus cum Tryphoni*, 80, 110)

- A few years after Justin died for his faith, Irenaeus of Lyons—a student of Polycarp, who had been a disciple of the apostle John—wrote that "ten kings shall give their kingdom to the beast and cause the church to flee.... After the antichrist has devastated all things in this world, he will reign for three years and six months." (Irenaeus, *Adversus Haereses*, 5:26:1; 5:30:4)

- A generation after Irenaeus, Tertullian of Carthage declared that, near the end of time, "the beast antichrist will wage war on the church of God. ... We agree that a kingdom is promised to us on earth, before heaven." (Tertullian, *Adversus Marcionem*, 3:25; Tertullian, *De Resurrectione Carnis*, 25)

Historical premillennialism may or may not be the correct view of the end times—but it is clearly the most ancient view. Each of these ancient church leaders anticipated the return of Jesus and the resurrection of the dead to occur immediately before an earthly millennium. What's more, they also seem to have expected the church to endure the great tribulation. Later historical premillennialists have included Charles H. Spurgeon, Oswald J. Smith, Corrie Ten Boom, Harold Ockenga, Carl F.H. Henry, George Eldon Ladd, and David Dockery.

Simply because Christians endure the great tribulation does not mean, of course, that Christians will endure God's wrath during the great tribulation! Through his sufferings on the cross, Jesus has already endured God's wrath in place of every person who trusts in him; that's why Paul could so confidently declare that "God has not destined us for wrath" (1 Thessalonians 5:9). Christians will, however, endure the sufferings of the great tribulation in the form of pain and persecution, diseases and even natural disasters that God allows.

• Why is historical premillennialism known as "historical"?

_____

_____

_____

• What similarities do you see between dispensational premillennialism and historical premillennialism?

_____

_____

_____

• What differences do you see between dispensational premillennialism and historical premillennialism?

_____

_____

_____

One Plan, One People: What's Most Distinctive about Historical Premillennialism

The placement of the rapture after the great tribulation is not, however, the only difference between historical and dispensational perspectives. In fact, the timing of the rapture isn't even the most important distinction between these viewpoints! The deepest divergence between dispensational and historical premillennialists has to do with how each group views the relationship between the nation of Israel and the church. Dispensational premillennialists organize God's work into dispensations. In each dispensation, God works in a particular way with a particular people. God's activities with Israel and with the church occur— according to dispensationalists—as parts of two different dispensations.

Historical premillennialists take a very different viewpoint on how God has worked with Israel and the church. From a historical premillennial perspective, God has always had one plan and one people. God's plan has always been to create one people for his glory through the death and resurrection of Jesus. All of God's work with the nation of Israel in the Hebrew Scriptures was simply preparation for the coming of Jesus and for the fulfillment of God's promises through the church. Both in the New Testament and in the Old, it was only through faith in Jesus that anyone could enter into a relationship with God. God's true people in every age have been those who live by faith in Jesus as the divine Messiah-King. Before Jesus arrived on earth, people trusted in Jesus by looking expectantly for a Messiah who was yet to come (Hebrews 11:13, 39–40).

	The Nation of Israel	The Church
Historical Premillennialism	God has always had one plan and one people. God's work with the nation of Israel was preparatory for his revelation of himself through Jesus and his work with the church.	It is through Jesus and through the church that God is fulfilling the promises that he made to the patriarchs and to the people of Israel. In the Old Testament and the New, God's plan has always been to redeem every person who trusts in God's Messiah. Jesus came to accomplish this redemption through his death and resurrection.
Dispensational Premillennialism	God has purposed to work with two different groups of people—Israel and the church—in different dispensations. God will fulfill his promises to the patriarchs and to the people of Israel through the modern nation of Israel.	The church is a parenthesis within God's work with the political nation of Israel. During the great tribulation, God will remove the church from the world and continue his work with the nation of Israel.

But What about God's Promise to Abraham?

At this point, you may be asking some quite good questions about historical premillennialism—questions like these: "Didn't God choose the offspring of Abraham for a special purpose? If God has always had one plan and one people, what about God's promises of land to Abraham? Has God rejected the Jewish people?"

Nearly every historical premillennialist would respond that God has not rejected the Jewish people. The Jews are, after all, beloved by God "for the sake of their forefathers" (Romans 11:28). At the same time, historical premillennialists do understand God's fulfillment of his promises to Israel in a slightly different way than dispensationalists. From a historical premillennial perspective, God's primary purpose when he chose Abraham was for the children of Abraham to be the people through whom Jesus came into the world. Even then, God intended his promises to Abraham and to the Israelites to find their fulfillment in Jesus.

As proof of this pattern, historical premillennialists point to these words from the apostle Paul: "The promises were made to Abraham and to his offspring. It does not say, 'And to offsprings,' referring to many, but referring to one, 'And to your offspring,' who is Christ" (Galatians 3:16). God's promise to give Abraham all the land from the Nile River to the Euphrates River (Genesis 15:18) will be fulfilled—but not because the modern nation of Israel will somehow gain this land! The promises were made primarily to Jesus ("to one," Galatians 3:16). During the millennial kingdom, Jesus will reign from Jerusalem not only over the land promised to Abraham but also over the whole earth. And so, during the millennium, Jesus will fulfill God's promise that Abraham's offspring would gain the land from the Nile to the Euphrates far beyond Israel's grandest expectations. Baptist theologian Russell Moore puts it this way: "Dispensationalists are right that only ethnic Jews receive the promised future restoration, but Paul makes clear that the 'seed of Abraham' is singular, not plural (Galatians 3:16). ... Does this promise apply to ethnic Jews? Yes, one ethnic Jew whose name is Jesus." (R. Moore, "Is There a Future for Israel?" http://www.russellmoore.com/2009/01/09/is-there-a-future-for-israel/)

What, then, does the future hold for the Jewish people, according to historical premillennialists? At some point before the return of Jesus, historical premillennialists anticipate widespread spiritual awakening among the Jewish people. Jews throughout the world will turn to Jesus as their Messiah, their

Savior, and their God. That's what Paul was predicting when he wrote that Israel would remain resistant to the gospel only "until the fullness of the Gentiles has come in" (Romans 11:25). For historical premillennialists, the primary inheritance and the focus of God's promise is not the physical land of Israel but the divine person of Jesus. And so, what historical premillennialists anticipate is not a restoration of the modern nation of Israel to their land but a turning of Jewish people to Jesus. Because of this expectation, there is every reason to proclaim the good news about Jesus "to the Jew first" (Romans 1:16).

- Carefully study Galatians 3:6–16, looking at the role of Jesus in fulfilling God's promise to Abraham. How do historical premillennialists understand these verses?

_____

_____

_____

- List three questions that you have about the historical premillennial perspective:

1. _____

2. _____

3. _____

Now, let's take a look at a few verses from Revelation to see more clearly how historical premillennialists view the works of God leading up to the end of time.

ℭ Look up and read Revelation 7:1–8

Ever since John walked through a door in the heavens, everything that he has seen has revolved around the glorious throne of God (Revelation 4:1–2). Now, John's attention is drawn earthward again. John sees "four angels, standing at the four corners of the earth"—perhaps representing all the powers of creation itself, under the power of God. Then, rising like the sun in the eastern sky, John glimpses an angel who holds "the seal of the living God."

The "seal of the living God" suggests the mark or impression of a king's signet ring. A signet-sealed letter from a king must remain intact until the document reaches the desired location. Likewise, God's seal upon these people represents a promise that they will persevere until they reach God's goal for his people. Later in Revelation, the seal is revealed to be the very name of God himself (Revelation 14:1).

A protective mark or seal was a familiar metaphor in the minds of John's readers. The idea of a mark to distinguish God's people appeared frequently in ancient Jewish literature. In one of Ezekiel's visions, God commanded a mark to be placed on the foreheads of those who had rejected the wickedness around them. This mark symbolized God's preservation of those who were faithful (Ezekiel 9:4–6). Other Jewish and Christian writings also picked up on the idea of a symbolic mark or seal. A Jewish psalm written a few years before the birth of Jesus declared, "The mark of God is on the righteous so that they will be saved, ... but lawless people will not escape God's judgment. The mark of destruction is on their foreheads." *(Psalms of Solomon 15:6–9)*. The apostle Paul used this sort of language in the New Testament, describing Christians as people as "sealed" by the Holy Spirit (2 Corinthians 1:22; Ephesians 1:13; 4:30). In the early second century, a pastor named Ignatius of Antioch wrote, "There are two coinages.... Each has its appropriate stamp impressed on it: Unbelievers bear the mark of this world; the faithful in love bear the mark of God." (Ignatius of Antioch, *Magnesieusin Ignatios*, 5). Another text places these words in the mouth of the Messiah: "I recognized [my people] and imprinted a seal on their faces.... They will not be deprived of my name." *(Odes of Solomon, 8:13, 19.)*

In all of these instances, it is clear that the seal on the forehead was not intended as a physical mark. The sealing of the 144,000 is not a physical marking of these people; the sealing symbolizes God's guarantee that this group will endure to the end. This does not mean that these people will escape suffering. What it means is that God will sustain them, even through persecution, until they reach the destination that God has decreed for them.

- Scan Genesis 49 and Ezekiel 48. Focus on the listing of the sons or tribes of Israel in each chapter. Compare the lists in Genesis and Ezekiel with the list in Revelation 7. What are the similarities between Genesis, Ezekiel, and Revelation? What are the differences?

_____

_____

_____

The Search for the 144,000

But who are the people in this God-marked multitude of 144,000? Dispensationalists have typically understood the 144,000 to be Jewish believers—12,000 from each tribe—preserved by God to be witnesses during the great tribulation. But historical premillennialists—as well as amillennialists and postmillennialists—see shortcomings in this interpretation. Here's why: John and his readers certainly knew the lists of Israel's tribes in the Hebrew Scriptures; yet, John was inspired by the Holy Spirit to record a different list than any of the listings that appear in the Hebrew Scriptures—and in a very different order! John's list is not the same as the list of Jacob's sons that appears in Genesis. Neither is it the listing of tribal territories from the prophecies of Ezekiel.

Why did God guide John to record such a distinct listing? Historical premillennialists understand this deliberate divergence from the Old Testament listings to be an inspired hint, intended to show readers that John meant the list in Revelation to be taken as a symbol of something other than the earthly nation of Israel.

The 12 Sons of Jacob (Genesis 49)	The 12 Tribal Territories (Ezekiel 48)	The 12 Tribes in Revelation (Revelation 7)
Reuben	Dan	Judah
Simeon	Asher	Reuben
Levi	Naphtali	Gad
Judah	Manasseh	Asher
Zebulun	Ephraim	Naphtali
Issachar	Reuben	Manasseh
Dan	Judah	Simeon
Gad	Benjamin	Levi
Asher	Simeon	Issachar
Naphtali	Issachar	Zebulun
Joseph	Zebulun	Joseph
Benjamin	Gad	Benjamin

So, if John's list does not refer to twelve physical tribes of the nation of Israel, what might the list mean?

The 144,000 are the church on earth; they represent the full number of those who endure tribulation.

According to historical premillennialists, this fits very well with other descriptions of the church throughout the New Testament:

- James addressed believers in Jesus as "the twelve tribes" (James 1:1; 2:1); so, first-century Christians clearly understood "the twelve tribes" to be a rightful way of referring to believers in Jesus.

- Paul understood the church to be the consummation of God's work with Israel. Paul could declare that God would save "all Israel" (Romans 9:6; 11:26) because the true Israel in every age has included every person—Jew or Gentile—who trusts in God's Messiah.

- Paul even referred to Christians as "the Israel of God" (Galatians 6:16; see also Philippians 3:3).

- Based on Scriptures such as these, historical premillennialists understand "144,000" as a reference to the church on earth during the great tribulation. The 144,000 are the great multitude of men and women who have heard the message first proclaimed by the apostles and who have trusted Jesus as the fulfillment of God's work with the tribes of Israel. This does not mean, of course, that only 144,000 people will be saved! The number 144,000 is an important symbol. The number of the tribes of Israel (12) multiplied by the number of the apostles (12) represents the people of God in their fullness, while 1,000—ten to the third power—depicts the great magnitude of God's people.

- How do historical premillennialists explain the differences between the listing of tribes in Revelation and the Old Testament lists?

_____

_____

_____

- What might the number 144,000 mean, according to historical premillennialists?

_____

ℭ Look up and read Revelation 7:9–14

If the 144,000 represent the people of God on earth during the great tribulation, what about the great multitude in Revelation 7? Who are these people "from all tribes and people and languages"? Why did John see them around the throne of God? If you aren't quite certain, don't feel bad: When one of the elders asked John who they were, the apostle himself wasn't completely certain at first! In response, the elder provided this answer: "These are the ones coming out of the great tribulation."

From the perspective of historical premillennialists—as well as many amillennialists and postmillennialists—the great multitude "coming out of the great tribulation" is the same group as the 144,000, described from a different vantage point. The 144,000 are the church on earth during the great tribulation. The great multitude is God's church glimpsed from the viewpoint of eternity, after every tribulation has ended.

Remember, John saw these visions from a perspective outside of time and space. So, it was entirely possible for him to hear about the church enduring tribulation and then immediately see the church triumphant after the great tribulation!

John recorded a similar pattern once before in the book of Revelation: In chapter 5, John heard about Jesus as the triumphant Lion in (5:5) then he saw Jesus as the sacrificial Lamb (5:6). The same Savior is described using two different symbols. Likewise, in Revelation 7, the church is both the 144,000 sealed in verse 4 and the great multitude saved in verse 9. The same people are described from two different perspectives.

- Carefully study Revelation 5. Notice how Jesus is identified as the triumphant Lion and yet he is seen as the sacrificial Lamb. Spend some time meditating on the glory of Jesus. Write your reflections below:

_____

_____

_____

- Review Revelation 7. How is it possible that the 144,000 entering the great tribulation are the same group as the great multitude coming out of the great tribulation?

_____

_____

_____

What Jesus Said about the Great Tribulation

℟ *Look up and read Matthew 24:15–31*
(Also see parallel passages Mark 13:14–27 and Luke 21:20–28)

After pronouncing woe after woe upon the Pharisees, Jesus cried out, "All these things will come upon this generation. O Jerusalem, Jerusalem!" (Matthew 23:36–37). As Jesus turned to leave the temple, his disciples looked around them and declared, "What wonderful stones and what wonderful buildings!"—as if they thought this temple would last forever. Jesus replied darkly, "Not one stone will be left upon another that will not be thrown down." Once the disciples reached the Mount of Olives, Jesus predicted a great tribulation "such as has not been from the beginning of the world" (Matthew 24:21; Mark 13:1).

Historical premillennialists believe that the church remains on earth during the great tribulation. But what, from a historical premillennial perspective, happens during this time of trials and trouble? And how long does the great tribulation last? Some historical premillennialists understand the great tribulation as a relatively brief time-period—perhaps seven years or even three and one half years—that will occur near the end of time. Other historical premillennialists take the great tribulation to be a long time-period that began in the first century and continues until the end of time. Despite this difference, historical premillennialists agree on this central affirmation: Even in this time of tribulation, God preserves those who truly belong to him.

Timing the Tribulation:
Two Historical Premillennial Possibilities

	Brief tribulation near the end of time	Extended tribulation from the first century until Jesus returns
What is "the abomination of desolations" that Jesus predicted? (Matthew 24:15)	A future blasphemous act, perhaps committed by the Antichrist against Israel or the church. Antichrist may be understood as a specific political ruler who governs during the great tribulation.	The defilement of the Jewish temple, when Roman soldiers entered Jerusalem in AD 70 then burned and pillaged the temple. Antichrist represents the powers in every age—including the Roman emperors who demanded worship for themselves—that war against the power, purposes, and people of God.
Who was Jesus warning when he said "let those who are in Judea flee to the mountains"? (Matthew 24:16)	Future believers during the great tribulation	Past believers who were living near Jerusalem when Jesus spoke these words, who might be caught in the terrible wrath of the Roman army
How does the great tribulation described by Jesus relate to the 42 months of tribulation described by John in Revelation? (Matthew 24:21; Revelation 11:2; 13:5).	The great tribulation described by Jesus is the same as the time of tribulation described in Revelation. Forty-two months refers to 3½ years (if the two references in Revelation refer to the same time-period) or to seven years (if the references in Revelation refer to two time-periods that occur immediately after one another). This future great tribulation may also be the 70th week described in Daniel 9:24-27. For believers today, the great tribulation is yet to come.	The great tribulation described by Jesus is the same as the time of tribulation described in Revelation. Forty-two months refers to a long period of tribulation. The number is probably drawn from the 42 encampments of Israel in the wilderness (Numbers 33:5–29) and the 42 months of drought during the ministry of Elijah (Luke 4:25; James 5:17). The great tribulation began with the Jewish-Roman War (AD 66–73) or with the persecution of Christians under Nero (AD 64–68). In those events, the powers of this world set themselves against Jesus and against his people. The 70th week described in Daniel 9:24–27 was fulfilled during the Jewish-Roman War. Believers today are living in the great tribulation. The great tribulation will continue and worsen until Jesus returns.

	Brief tribulation near the end of time	**Extended tribulation from the first century until Jesus returns**
Where is the church during the great tribulation? (Matthew 24:21–31)	The church is the elect (Matthew 24:22–31. Compare 2 Timothy 2:10). During the great tribulation, the church endures persecution on the earth but is divinely protected from falling away.	The church is the elect (Matthew 24:22–31. Compare 2 Timothy 2:10). During the great tribulation, the church endures persecution on the earth but is divinely protected from falling away.
What will happen at the end of the great tribulation? (Matthew 24:29–31)	Immediately after the great tribulation, cosmic upheavals will accompany the return of Jesus. Just as citizens in ancient times ran out to meet their king as he approached their city, the church will be caught up to meet Jesus in the air and then immediately return with him to the earth.	Immediately after the great tribulation, cosmic upheavals will accompany the return of Jesus. Just as citizens in ancient times ran out to meet their king as he approached their city, the church will be caught up to meet Jesus in the air and then immediately return with him to the earth.

- Read Matthew 24:1–31. What in this text might suggest that Christians remain on the earth during the great tribulation?

  _____

  _____

  _____

- Carefully study the "Timing the Tribulation" chart. What are the key differences between the two perspectives on the great tribulation?

  _____

  _____

  _____

- Review Revelation 11–13, especially 11:2 and 13:5. Do you understand these two references to 42 months to be (1) figurative references to one extended time of tribulation, (2) the same 42 months, mentioned twice, or (3) two successive times of tribulation, for a total of seven years?

_____

_____

_____

Two Witnesses

Revelation 11:3–4 tells of two specific witnesses. Here are four possible understandings: (1) Some dispensational premillennialists see them as Moses and Elijah, brought back from the dead to testify to the truth of Jesus. (2) Others take the two witnesses to be two people like Moses and Elijah whom God will raise up to proclaim the gospel to the Jewish people near the end of time. (3) Still others understand them as symbols of the testimony of the church during times of tribulation. (4) Might represent the two primary divisions of the Hebrew Scriptures: the Law of Moses and the Prophets. The Law and Prophets testify to the truth of Jesus (Luke 24:44; Acts 28:23), the Jewish people have rejected this testimony (2 Corinthians 3:14–16), but the day will come when God breathes new life into this testimony and brings spiritual awakening to Jewish people.

You may not accept a historical premillennial perspective on the end times—and, if you don't, that's okay! Even if you don't believe that the church will endure the great tribulation, historical premillennialism reminds us about how God constantly uses day-by-day tribulations to move his people toward maturity.

That's why, according to the apostle Paul, Christians must not merely tolerate the tribulations of this life—Christians should see tribulations as opportunities for God to purify and to transform his people (Romans 5:3–5; 12:12; 2 Corinthians 6:4–5). Barnabas and Paul testified together that it is only "through many tribulations that we enter God's kingdom" (Acts 14:22). Paul even declared that Christians are "destined" for tribulation (1 Thessalonians 3:3). Jesus predicted that believers would endure tribulation

God grows his people through trials and tribulations. Historical premillennialism emphasizes God's preservation of his people through suffering and tribulation.

(John 16:21–22) and made it clear that his followers would be "in the world" during at least some times of tribulation (John 16:33).

The End is Near

And so, with this survey of historical premillennialism, our exploration of the end times comes to an end. Think back to when you began this study. Have you arrived at a different perspective on the end times than you had at the beginning? Are you convinced even more strongly of the viewpoint that you've always held? Or do you need to engage in deeper study as you reconsider what you believe about the end times?

Regardless of your view of the end times, what I want to leave you with is the same simple truth that John was inspired to write at the end of Revelation: "May the grace of our Lord Jesus Christ be with you all" (22:21).

If your study has led you to obsess over details of the end times or to criticize Christians who hold different viewpoints, you have wasted your time—the closing verses of Revelation call us to grace, not self-righteousness. A God-centered study of the end times should lead you closer to our Lord Jesus Christ and deeper into fellowship with other believers ("with you all")—even if those believers disagree with you when it comes to the details of how God will end the world! Jesus is, after all, the goal and the endpoint of God's work in history, and Jesus calls us to live in community with everyone who trusts in him.

What's more, all four views of the end times unite around these essential truths: Jesus is returning, and only those who trust in him will share in his eternal glory. Which leaves us with this crucial question: Where do you stand with Jesus? If you are uncertain whether you have truly trusted Jesus, search your innermost desires. Do you despise your sin? Do you want to love God above all other things? Do you long to be obedient to Jesus? Trust Jesus now as the Master of your life and as the Living Lord of all Creation! Recognize his suffering on the cross as God's substitute for the punishment that you deserve. And then, cry out with the author of Revelation, "Even so, come, Lord Jesus!" (Revelation 22:20).

Now What?

PRAY: Almighty Lord, as we earnestly wait for your coming, protect us from falling into sin. When you return and our longings are fulfilled, we long to be pardoned and pure before you. Grant this, our plea, in the name of the Blessed One who lives and reigns forever. Amen. (Adapted from Apringius of Beja's *Studies in Revelation*, mid-sixth century)

LEARN: Study Revelation 20, 21, and 22. Memorize Revelation 21:1–4.

DO: You have gained much knowledge about the end times—and this knowledge may be dangerous to your spiritual health! Here's why: Without love, knowledge leads to self-righteous pride (1 Corinthians 8:1–3). Examine your attitudes carefully. Have you developed a prideful attitude about your knowledge? Has your knowledge caused you to become critical of fellow-believers in Jesus? Have you left behind the love that you had at first? Meditate on Revelation 2:1–7, especially verses 4 and 5. Ask God to shatter your self-righteousness. If necessary, ask forgiveness from people whom you have criticized.

Notes

Notes

Notes

Christianity, Cults & Religions
DVD-Based Study
For Individual or Group Use

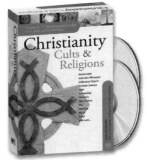

Complete *Christianity, Cults & Religions* DVD-Based Study Kit
• Contains one each of everything below
  ISBN: 9781596364134

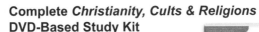

Christianity, Cults & Religions DVD-Based Study Leader Pack
• All six DVD-based sessions
• Leader Guide on disc as a printable PDF
• Fliers, bulletin inserts, posters & banners as PDFs on disc
  ISBN: 9781596364271

Leader Guide
• Leader Guide gives step-by-step instructions for group hosts or facilitators so you don't have to be the expert
  ISBN: 9781596364288

Participant Guide
• Each participant will need a guide
• Guide contains definitions, charts, comparisons, Bible references, discussion questions, and more
  ISBN: 9781596364295

Pamphlet – fold-out chart
• Side-by-side comparison chart compares 21 groups
• 14-panel chart fits in the back of a Bible cover
• Perfect for quick reference when cultists come to the door
• Contains Scripture references to support Christian beliefs
  ISBN: 9789901981403

PowerPoint® presentation
• Contains more than 200 slides to expand the scope of the teaching
  ISBN: 9781890947323

Christianity, Cults & Religions handbook - 112 pages
• Full color handbook is perfect for quick reference on more than 40 groups
• In-depth analysis of Jehovah's Witnesses, Mormonism, Islam, Buddhism, Hinduism and more
• Contains Scripture references to support Christian beliefs
• Includes 10 Keys for Witnessing to Cults
• Includes sections on Freemasonry, Kabbalah Centre, Wicca, Nation of Islam and more
  ISBN: 9781596362024

christianitycultsandreligions.com

Other Products from Rose Publishing

Bible Reference Made Easy

Books, maps,
fold-out pamphlets,
Bible studies,
wall charts,
PowerPoint®
presentations

Hundreds of reproducible charts!

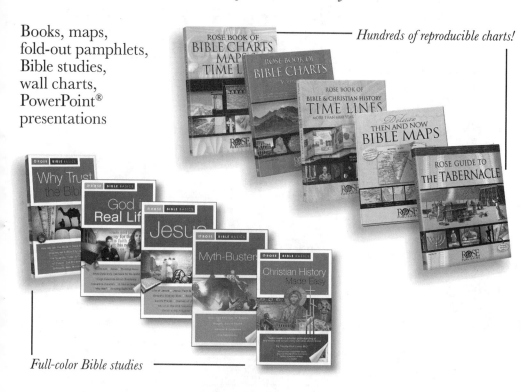

Full-color Bible studies

Fold-out pamphlets
These high-gloss plastic-coated
fact sheets contain hundreds of
facts and fit inside the cover of
most Bibles. They include the
most important information on
the topic at a glance.

Full-color wall charts

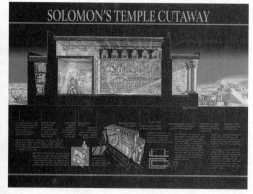

PUBLISHING
www.rose-publishing.com

Found wherever good Christian books are sold.